Corporate Acquisitions and Mergers in Cambodia

Corporate Acquisitions and Mergers in Cambodia

Chris Robinson

DFDL

This book was originally published as a chapter in Corporate Acquisitions and Mergers.

General Editor: Peter Begg

Wolters Kluwer

Published by:
Kluwer Law International B.V.
PO Box 316
2400 AH Alphen aan den Rijn
The Netherlands
E-mail: lrs-sales@wolterskluwer.com
Website: www.wolterskluwer.com/en/solutions/kluwerlawinternational

Sold and distributed by:
Wolters Kluwer Legal & Regulatory U.S.
920 Links Avenue
Landisville, PA 17538
United States of America
E-mail: customer.service@wolterskluwer.com

ISBN 978-94-035-3017-8

e-Book: ISBN 978-94-035-3027-7
web-PDF: ISBN 978-94-035-3037-6

Contents

DFDL

DFDL was established in 1994 and founded on a unique vision: to create an integrated legal and tax advisory firm, with in-depth knowledge of the jurisdictions where we are based. Our dedicated professionals possess the acumen and insight necessary to assist you in navigating the legal complexities and challenges that investors encounter when doing business in this region. Drawing on our wide-ranging industry experience and finely-tuned local knowledge of the countries where DFDL operates, we strive to provide concise, commercially focused and innovative advice tailored specifically to the matter or transaction at hand and our clients' needs. DFDL has offices throughout Southeast and South Asia, including collaborating firms, in Bangladesh, Cambodia, Indonesia, Lao PDR, Myanmar, Philippines, Singapore, Thailand and Vietnam.

DFDL is organized into regional practice groups that operate across our offices. These practice areas reflect our core expertise and the major industry sectors that we focus on, specifically:

- corporate/M&A;
- equity capital markets;
- banking and finance;
- employment;
- dispute resolution and investigations;
- energy, mining and infrastructure;
- real estate and construction;
- taxation;
- accounting and customs;
- technology;
- media and telecommunications; and
- intellectual property.

DFDL Cambodia established its office in Phnom Penh in January 1995 as the first officially authorized foreign investment advisory and tax firm in Cambodia.

DFDL Cambodia received Tier 1 ranking for Financial & Corporate from IFLR 1000 in 2021. DFDL Cambodia was also ranked as the National Firm of the year 2021 by IFLR. DFDL was also named Mekong Region Law Firm of the Year 2021 by Chambers Asia Pacific.

Author

This country chapter on Corporate M&A in Cambodia has been written by the following team of professionals and consultants from DFDL Cambodia's office: Chris Robinson, Robin Teow, Clint O'Connell, Vansok Khem, Sophorne Kheang, Samnangvathana Sor, Leab Seng, Raksa Chan, Sophal Yun, Davy Kong, Simon Burlinson and David Fruitman. This chapter was reviewed and coordinated by Chris Robinson and Simon Burlinson.

If you have any queries, please contact:

Chris Robinson

Partner

E-mail: chris.robinson@dfdl.com

1 CAMBODIA: ECONOMIC, POLITICAL AND CULTURAL BACKGROUND

1.1 Population, Language and Currency

[01] Cambodia, officially known as the Kingdom of Cambodia, is located in the southern portion of the Indochina Peninsula in Southeast Asia. Covering 181 035 sq. km., the country is bordered by Thailand to the northwest, Lao PDR to the northeast, Vietnam to the east, and the Gulf of Thailand to the southwest.

[02] The population of Cambodia has grown rapidly since the end of the Khmer Rouge Regime in 1979 to around 16.718 million people. The largest city is the capital Phnom Penh, with an estimated population of approximately 2.2 million. Phnom Penh has been the national capital since the French colonization of Cambodia. It has grown to become the core area of economic and industrial activity in the country, as well as the center of security, politics, cultural heritage, and diplomacy.

[03] Belonging to the Austro-Asiatic family of languages, Khmer is the national language of Cambodia. Most social contexts such as government administration, education at all levels, and the mass media use the Khmer language. As Cambodia is a former French colony, French remains popular among the older generation. It is English, however, that remains by far the most popular and widely spoken foreign language throughout the country with use of Mandarin becoming more prevalent.

[04] The Cambodian Riel, abbreviated as KHR, is the official currency in Cambodia, although the US dollar is in wide circulation, generally accepted everywhere and easily exchanged. The exchange rate is USD1 to approximately KHR4 100.

1.2 Government and Political System

[05] Under the 1993 constitution, Cambodia is a constitutional monarchy with the King as its head of state. The King represents a symbol of unity and eternity of the nation. The state power is divided into three branches:

(i) Legislative power: The main responsibility of the legislature is to create the laws and regulations. There is a bicameral parliament which consists of the senate and the national assembly.

(ii) Executive power: The executive branch, called the Royal Government of Cambodia, includes the Prime Minister, the Council of Ministers, the ministries, provincial and municipal authorities, and other government agencies. The current head of government is Prime Minister Hun Sen, who has been in power since 1985.

(iii) Judicial power: At present, the Cambodian judiciary consists of one Supreme Court, one Appellate Court, and provincial/municipal courts. Many courts of first instance are located in each province and municipality, and the Military

Court as well as the hybrid court which is known as the Extraordinary Chambers in the Courts of Cambodia.

[06] In the 2018 elections, the Cambodian People's Party (CPP) won all of the 125 seats in the National Assembly. His Excellency Samdech Hun Sen returned to office as the Prime Minister on Friday, August 17, 2018. The political situation in Cambodia remains stable.

[07] The next national election will be held in 2023.

[08] Cambodia is a Member State of the World Trade Organization (WTO) having ratified the WTO agreements in 2004 and acceded to the constitutive WTO Agreement and covered agreements on trade, services, intellectual property and various other topics.

[09] Accession to the WTO has had a significant impact on all sectors and fields of business in Cambodia. The most significant effects of WTO accession relate to:

(i) the adoption of a broader legal framework;
(ii) WTO agreements superseding national law;
(iii) Cambodia's commitment to the liberalization of services and tariffs;
(iv) the improvement of judicial and quasi-judicial processes; and
(v) the supranational jurisdiction of the WTO Court.

1.3 ASEAN and AEC

[10] With foreign direct investment (FDI) in Southeast Asia reaching about USD1373 billion in 2020, the Association of Southeast Asian Nations (ASEAN), taken as a whole, remains one of the world's most dynamic markets, with direct investment from outside and within the region. Despite the COVID-19 pandemic that adversely affected the entire ASEAN region, there has been optimism that the economies of ASEAN will recover faster than expected. According to the Asian Development Bank, ASEAN's GDP growth rate is expected to reach 4.7% in 2022 and 4.5% in 2023 due to more effective virus containment and the return of broad-based economic activity. Although ASEAN's total trade value decreased by around 5.5% in 2020, there was a rise in demand for electronics, electrical machinery, furniture, and bedding materials. To ensure that the ASEAN economy will recover, all Southeast Asian nations, including Cambodia, need to formulate strategies to remain sustainable and resilient across all of their sectors.[1]

1.4 Legal System

[11] Although, conceptually, Cambodia is a civil law country, its legal system and legal institutions can present a somewhat complex labyrinth for foreign investors to

[1] The ASEAN Economic Integration Brief—(These can be seen in ASEAN Integration Report 2021).

navigate. The situation, however, is improving following the accession of Cambodia to the WTO and the passing of several key commercial laws. The new laws and regulations combine aspects of the pre-1975 French Civil Code system with legal principles from common law systems. Also, Cambodia is particularly interested in ensuring that its legal system integrates successfully with those of the other members of ASEAN.

[12] The National Assembly has adopted numerous laws since it was formed in 1993. Some significant examples include the Law on Commercial Enterprises (LCE), equivalent to a "company law" or "corporation law" in other jurisdictions, and the Investment Law, as well as the Law on Negotiable Instruments and Payment Transactions, the Secured Transactions Law, the Civil Code, the Customs Law, the Law on Standards, the Insolvency Law, the Anti-Corruption Law (ACL), the Expropriation Law and the Law on Anti-Money Laundering and Combating Terrorism Financing (AMLCTF).

[13] Other important laws have also been enacted during the past decade, such as the Law on Issuance and Trading of Government Securities, the Law on Issuance and Trading of Non-Government Securities, the Commercial Arbitration Law, the Telecommunication Law, the Commercial Remedy Law, the Trust Law, the Consumer Protection Law, the Competition Law, the New Law on Investment, and the E-Commerce Law. Further laws are expected soon, including the Commercial Contract Law, as well as many other laws touching on nearly all aspects of business activity, which are being drafted by various ministries with the technical assistance of several donor countries. Interestingly, Cambodian regulators are working to put in place key regulations in the technology and fund management sectors, including the issuance of the collective investment schemes regulation and drafting of cryptocurrencies' trading regulation.

[14] Although Cambodia's ongoing transformation into a free market system has resulted in many new laws and regulations being passed, new policies being implemented, and refinement of the judicial institutions, the legal framework is still developing. The implementation and enforcement of existing laws can be subject to the discretion of governmental authorities. However, Cambodia's progress in easing entry into the market, doing business, and resolving commercial disputes, continues its gradual and methodical path towards improvement.

[15] Laws are enforced through the Cambodian court system. To many foreign investors, Cambodian courts are still generally considered complex and unpredictable. The mandatory use of the local Khmer language adds an additional barrier to foreign investors. As a result, Cambodian courts are often not the preferred forum for resolving commercial disputes by foreign investors, yet they are in the best position to enforce judgments against Cambodian companies. As a civil law jurisdiction, court judgments do not tend to be binding in subsequent cases.

[16] In 2013, Cambodia entered into its first agreement for the mutual recognition of civil court judgments with Vietnam called the "Cambodia-Vietnam Judicial Assistance Treaty." Such treaty covers various issues for civil matters, including the service of judicial documents, the summoning of witnesses and, importantly, the recognition and enforcement of court judgments. In the absence of agreements for the mutual recognition of civil court judgments with other countries, it is unlikely that other foreign court judgments would be enforced in Cambodia.

1.5 Current Economic Aspects

[17] Despite witnessing vigorous economic growth over the past two decades, Cambodia's economy unfortunately suffered from a contraction in 2020 due to the COVID-19 pandemic. Notwithstanding, Cambodia is recovering well, such as agriculture, manufacturing, and retail, although certain sectors, particularly tourism and hospitality, are recovering at a slower pace. According to the Asian Development Bank, Cambodia's economy is forecast to grow by 5.3% in 2022. According to the Asian Development Outlook, industrial production will increase by approximately 8.1% in 2022 driven by a gradual recovery in the garment, footwear, travel goods, electronics and bicycle manufacturing sectors. The real estate and construction industry is expected to continue to grow in 2022, although at a slower rate than in recent years.

1.6 Openness to Foreign Investment

[18] Investment in Cambodia is, in most cases, a straightforward, direct, and open process. All sectors of the economy are open to foreign investment, and the government permits 100% foreign ownership of companies in most sectors. There is little or no discrimination against foreign investors either at the time of initial investment or after investment. The business-friendly government, the widespread use and acceptance of USD, non-restricted foreign exchange (except in limited circumstances), a favorable tax regime and investment incentives are significant advantages of doing business in Cambodia.

[19] Cambodia received FDI inflows of around USD4 35 billion in 2021, a 22% increase from the preceding year. To ensure that FDI inflows are sustained in the upcoming years, Cambodia has signed various bilateral investment and taxation treaties. By 2020, Cambodia had signed bilateral investment treaties with twenty-seven countries and numerous regional investment agreements. Additionally, the nation has secured double taxation agreements with several countries, including Singapore, China, Hong Kong Special Administrative Region, Macau Special Administrative Region, Brunei, Thailand, Vietnam, Malaysia, the Republic of Korea, Indonesia and Turkey.

Cambodia has recently enacted a new competition law and a new investment law, which are hoped to make it more attractive for foreign companies to invest in Cambodia in the upcoming years. The investment climate in the nation should also be enhanced by Cambodia's ongoing efforts to provide investment incentives for foreign investors and build more special economic zones and foreign trade zones. These details help showcase Cambodia as a favorable nation for other countries to place their investments, despite the unpredictable situation of the COVID-19 pandemic.

1.7 Cultural Aspects

[20] In Cambodia, greetings between local people depend on the relationship, hierarchy and age. In the presence of a foreigner, however, Cambodian people have, for the most part, adopted western-style greetings and hand-shaking.

[21] In Cambodia, "yes" does not necessarily have the same meaning as in western countries. It does not often mean acceptance, and if a question has been asked, a "yes" does not mean that the person has understood. Rather, "yes" generally means that the person is listening to you. This cultural sensitivity issue can be confusing to foreigners and can lead to misunderstandings as to whether an agreement has been reached. It is important to read between the lines, especially the body language. In Cambodia, smiling can have several meanings such as friendliness, satisfaction or embarrassment. It is not common in Cambodia to express negative feelings (e.g., anger or nervousness) or direct negative feedback.

[22] When a misunderstanding is revealed, it is important not to overreact and keep in mind the cultural difference. The notion of loss of face is very important in Cambodia and avoiding loss of face is a starting point for a good relationship. It is offensive to criticize in public or disagree with direct negative feedback. These cultural differences can create embarrassment, loss of honor and thereafter, a complicated relationship.

2 REGULATORY FRAMEWORK

2.1 Overview of Corporate Law in Cambodia

[23] The incorporation of a company is mainly governed by: (i) the Law on Commercial Rules and Commercial Register, promulgated on June 19, 1995 (LCRCR); (ii) the Law on the Amendment of the Law on Commercial Rules and Commercial Register, promulgated on November 18, 1999 (LACRCR); (iii) the LCE, promulgated on June 19, 2005 and (iv) the Law on the Amendment to the Law on Commercial Enterprises, promulgated on January 29, 2022 (LALCE).

[24] The above legislation replaced the former practice of business structures operating on the basis of contractual arrangements. The LCRCR, LACRCR, LCE and LALCE provide a comprehensive framework to establish and operate various types of business organization forms.

[25] At present, the available forms of business entities in Cambodia are:

(i) limited liability company;
(ii) branch office;
(iii) representative office;

(iv) partnership; and
(v) sole proprietorship.

[26] There are three types of limited liability companies:

(i) single-member private limited company;
(ii) private limited company; and
(iii) public limited company.

[27] A partnership may take the form of a general partnership or a limited partnership.

2.2 Commercial Registration under the LCRCR and LACRCR

[28] The LCRCR and LACRCR provide an extensive procedure for registering an enterprise at the Ministry of Commerce (MOC). They set out the necessary documents required for the registration of a company or business and determine the circumstances whereby any changes in a company must be notified to the MOC.

[29] According to the LCRCR and LACRCR, the commercial register lists basic information on all registered business entities, including the company name, objectives, form of company, location of the registered office, capital, certificate of capital deposit issued by a bank, names of directors and shareholders, equity held by each shareholder and authorized signatories. Also listed are any patents, trademarks and copyrights owned by the business, and any judgments or judicial orders pronouncing the dissolution or the nullity of the company or declaring the company in bankruptcy or court-ordered liquidation.

[30] To better streamline the incorporation process and to provide easy access and transparency for both local and foreign investors, the MOC introduced, in mid-2020, a single portal online business registration system via which the registration process must now be conducted. The intention of this new online system is to automate registration with the MOC, the General Department of Taxation (GDT) and the Ministry of Labour and Vocational Training (MLVT)/Department of Labour and Vocational Training (DLVT) (for the declaration of opening the company), without filing separate applications. Other labor compliance processes required by the MLVT can also be performed online, albeit using a separate portal established by the MLVT. The initial registration with the NSSF is still undertaken offline (hard copy only).

2.3 LCE

[31] Under the LCE, enterprises must comply with several requirements, including, among other things:

(i) Agent.
A partnership or company must continuously maintain a registered agent that must be a legally competent natural person in Cambodia.

(ii) Registered office.
At all times, a company must have a registered office in Cambodia.

(iii) Issuance of shares.
Subject to industry-specific requirements, there is no longer a minimum capital requirement, although most companies continue to issue a minimum of 1 000 shares with a par value of KHR4 000 per share (approximately USD1).

(iv) Share certificates.
Each shareholder is entitled to a share certificate, upon shares being fully paid-up.

(v) Records.
Companies must prepare and maintain corporate records at the registered office, including:
(a) articles of incorporation (AOIs) and bylaws;
(b) minutes of meetings and resolutions of directors;
(c) copies of all notices;
(d) securities register;
(e) director records (including minutes of meetings);
(f) resolutions of shareholders; and
(g) accounting records.

(vi) Meetings of the board of directors.
Board of directors' meetings must be held at least once every three months.

(vii) Annual declaration.
Following the issuance of the Prakas by the MOC on April 5, 2017 regarding the filing of the Annual Declaration of Commercial Enterprises (ADCE), an ADCE must now be submitted by each enterprise to the MOC using its online system.
Use of the online system for submission of an ADCE is now compulsory and must be performed within three months from the anniversary of the enterprise's incorporation or, for companies registered prior to the introduction of the online system, re-registration on the MOC's online system. After this three-month period, a penalty of KHR2 million (approximately USD500) will be imposed by the MOC.

(viii) Annual financial statement.
Twenty-one days before each annual shareholders' meeting, an annual financial statement must be sent to all shareholders (unless a shareholder has informed the company in writing that it does not wish to receive a copy). Before being issued, published, and circulated, annual financial statements shall be approved by the board of directors, and, unless certain conditions are met by the company and the shareholders have waived the requirement to appoint an auditor, such approval shall have a copy of an auditor's report attached.

(ix) Disclosure of interests.
Directors and officers must disclose in writing their interests in relation to any contracts with the company, or any material interest in relation to such a contract.

(x) Procedures for shareholders' meetings and board of directors meetings.
The LCE provides for specific procedures (including quorum requirements and secret ballots), notification periods and information disclosure in relation to shareholders' meetings and directors' meetings.

(xi) Corporate secretary.
The LCE refers, in several provisions, to the use of a company secretary responsible for taking and keeping the minutes of the board of directors' meetings and sending copies of the minutes to all directors. In addition, the company secretary must prepare a written report of the written communications of the board and distribute this report to the directors.

(xii) Use of Khmer name.
All enterprises must display their name in the Khmer language. If the name is displayed in another language, the Khmer name must be placed above and be larger than the name in the other language. The Khmer name must appear on all seals, signs, letterhead, and all documents used for public purposes.

[32] Other key issues covered by the LCE include:

(i) appointment of auditors;
(ii) provisions in relation to the liquidation of a business; and
(iii) penalties applicable for breaches of the law.

2.4 Business Vehicles

[33] The major legal forms of companies are summarized in the table below, followed by a more detailed examination of each form:

Form	*Definition*	*Pros*	*Cons*
Limited Liability Company	– Company in which liability of shareholders is limited to capital contribution. – Includes single-member private limited liability company.	– Widely accepted. – Bare minimum initial capital requirement. – Acceptable as a CDC-approved Qualified Investment Project. – Flexible forms.	– Taxable activities in Cambodia. – Higher reporting and administration burden. – Approvals required for share transfers and changes of directors (amongst other amendments to the company).

Form	*Definition*	*Pros*	*Cons*
Branch Office	– Division of an offshore parent company.	– Simplified internal, legal, and accounting structure.	– Not acceptable for CDC investment projects. – Exposes principal to liabilities of branch. – Taxable activities in Cambodia. – No separate legal personality from its principal. – Business activities must align strictly with those of the parent
Representative Office	– Local representative of the parent company.	– Rapid approval with minimum legal documentation. – No taxable activities in Cambodia.	– Not acceptable for CDC investment projects. – Scope of permissible activities limited. – Cannot engage in business activities in Cambodia in its own capacity. – No separate legal personality from its principal.

2.4.1 Limited Liability Company

[34] A limited liability company is the most common form of investment vehicle in Cambodia. It is usually established as a subsidiary of an investor's offshore holding company. A limited liability company can be 100% Cambodian-owned, 100% foreign-owned, or have any combination of Cambodian or foreign shareholding, subject to certain restrictions.

[35] A limited liability company is formed with the registration of its AOIs at, and receipt of a certificate of incorporation from, the MOC. Any changes to the AOIs and other corporate documents must also be registered in a timely manner at the MOC to be valid.

[36] After establishment, a limited liability company must prepare and maintain, at its registered office, the following records:

(i) the AOIs and all amendments thereto;
(ii) minutes of meetings and resolutions of shareholders;
(iii) copies of all notices required to be sent or filed in accordance with the LCE;
(iv) a securities register; and
(v) accounting records.

[37] The company may have only one class of shares unless the AOIs specify other classes. Subject to differing class rights, shareholders have the right to vote at any meeting of the shareholders, receive any dividends declared by the company, and receive the remaining property of the company upon dissolution. If the AOIs provide for more than one class of shares, the rights of each class may (theoretically) be absolute, relative or contingent, and the rights, privileges, restrictions, and conditions attaching to the shares of each class must be detailed in the AOIs.

[38] Generally, limited liability companies are managed by a board of directors, and such management power is mostly free from shareholders' interference. Shareholders have the power to appoint and remove directors.

[39] The board of directors has broad powers to manage the business and affairs of the company, which powers include:

(i) appointment and removal of officers and fixing of their salaries;
(ii) issuance, re-issuance or sale of securities of the company;
(iii) adoption of resolutions; and
(iv) the giving of guarantees on behalf of the company.

[40] However, directors must act in good faith, within the scope of the business objectives of the company and the framework of the company's AOIs, as well as in compliance with applicable laws. In addition, directors are liable for complying with the relevant registration, filing and publication requirements of the company. Accounting books and records must be duly maintained at the registered office for at least ten years.

[41] At every annual shareholders' meeting, the directors must present an annual financial statement to the shareholders. Annual financial statements must be approved by the board of directors and be accompanied by the auditor's report (subject to the limited circumstances whereby appointment of an auditor may be waived by shareholder resolution) before being issued, published and circulated.

2.5 Types of Limited Liability Company

[42] Under the LCE, there are three types of limited liability companies. The table below sets out the general characteristics of each of these types of companies. The LCE describes in detail the distinction between these forms:

Form	*Characteristics*
Single-Member Private Limited Company	A private limited company with one physical or legal person as the shareholder. Requires a minimum of one director.
Private Limited Company	A limited liability company with two to thirty shareholders. Requires a minimum of one director. May have restrictions on transfer of each class of shares as provided for by the AOIs.
Public Limited Company	A limited liability company that is authorized by the LCE to issue securities to the public. Requires a minimum of three directors.

2.6 Branch Office

[43] A foreign or local entity may operate its business in Cambodia through a branch office. Although relatively common in the banking community, the government's policy, historically, was to limit branches to foreign investors that have executed contracts with the government.

[44] Such a limitation is not provided for under the current law. One notable consideration for branches is that the foreign parent company can be legally liable for the losses and debts of the branch. Branches cannot undertake Qualified Investment Projects (QIPs) and do not have a separate legal personality from their principal parent company.

2.7 Partnership

[45] A "general partnership" is a contract between one or more persons to combine their property, knowledge or activities to carry on business with a common view to profit. They are jointly and severally liable for the obligations of the partnership to third parties.

[46] A "limited partnership" is a contract of partnership between one or more general partners who are the sole persons authorized to administer and bind the partnership, and one or more limited partners, who are bound to contribute to the capital of the partnership. The general partners are jointly and severally liable for the debts of the partnership to third parties, whereas the limited partners are liable only to the extent of the sum of money or value of the property they agreed to contribute.

[47] While this form is common for local and small businesses, it is not commonly used for larger investments, as the processes used by the MOC for registering this business form are unclear given the lack of precedent to date.

2.8 Representative Office

[48] For some investors, the need to establish a subsidiary or branch of their offshore company, while foreseeable in the longer term, may not immediately be necessary. A more appropriate form may be that of the representative office. Representative offices are primarily designed to facilitate sourcing local goods and services, and collecting local information for the parent company. They also serve as a vehicle for promoting and marketing the offshore parent's products and services in Cambodia. They are, therefore, best suited to assist foreign principals wishing to gain entry into the Cambodian marketplace.

[49] A representative office is not intended to engage in active trading or provide services in Cambodia. It may not purchase, sell, or conduct any service or activity considered to be within the usual scope of the parent company's business. It also may not engage in manufacturing, processing or construction. Permitted activities include the right to employ local workers and to market products and services at trade fairs. The representative office may negotiate commercial contracts on behalf of its principal, but the contract must be entered into by the principal.

[50] The representative office is a non-taxable legal entity precisely because it is not permitted to engage in any sort of taxable activity. However, the representative office is required to register with the GDT, withhold taxes, including salary tax for salaries paid to its employees and to pay patent tax (PT) (an annual business tax). Representative offices cannot register for QIP status.

2.9 Restrictions on Foreign Shareholdings

[51] Cambodia places very few restrictions on the level of foreign participation in investments. As a result, a substantial proportion of investors choose to establish 100% foreign-owned limited companies. However, it should be noted that only a Cambodian company or a Cambodian national can own land and foreign ownership restrictions apply to certain sectors.

2.10 Required Government Approvals, Permits and Licenses

[52] Certain business sectors, such as banking, education, construction and real estate, financial leasing, insurance, medical and pharmaceutical, mining, oil and gas, telecommunications, tourism and investment advisory services require specialized licenses from various government entities.

2.11 Laws Affecting M&A

[53] There is no specific or detailed mergers and acquisitions regime, or a general regulatory regime applicable to acquisitions of companies incorporated in Cambodia. Mergers and acquisitions are regulated by sector-specific legislation, and regulatory practices and many of the existing provisions remain untested as mergers and acquisitions are relatively new in Cambodia. Further, in Cambodia, no legal distinction is made between friendly/agreed or hostile transactions.

[54] Despite the lack of specific laws and regulations regarding mergers and acquisitions, few restrictions and regulations have to be considered for specific sectors. Also, there are certain sectors restricted to foreigners for reasons of national security, social safety or national economic necessity.

[55] As a matter of practice, there are three types of transactions in Cambodia: (i) asset or business transfer; (ii) share purchase; and (iii) statutory merger. Each is discussed in greater detail below:

(i) Asset or business transfer

In an asset/business transfer arrangement, the selling company and the acquiring company enter into an asset/business transfer agreement. On the closing date, assets and/or business are transferred from the selling company to the buying company. Existing agreements and obligations to perform ongoing business should be transferred as agreed in the asset/business transfer agreement. Certain transfers of continuing obligations may require the use of transfer notices and consents.

Liabilities (including historical tax liabilities) that are not transferred to the acquiring company remain with the selling company. There are no formal statutory rules, other than tax principles, which govern asset/business transfers.

Where the business to be transferred is in a regulated industry, for example, a financial institution or telecommunications, approval of the relevant authority—the National Bank of Cambodia (NBC) for financial institutions and the Ministry of Post and Telecommunications of Cambodia (MPTC) for telecommunications—should be obtained. Where the business to be transferred needs licenses for its operations, approval of the concerned authority must be obtained. Further, where the business or assets of a QIP company are being transferred, consent or approval from the Council for the Development of Cambodia (CDC) is typically required.

(ii) Share purchase

In a share purchase arrangement, the buyer simply buys shares of the company to be acquired from the selling shareholder(s). Liabilities and obligations existing within the company whose shares are acquired remain the liability of the acquired company. Where the business of the acquired company is in a regulated industry, for example, a financial institution or telecommunications, or a QIP, approval of the relevant authorities concerned will be required. All share transfers must be registered with the MOC.

From a Cambodian tax perspective, if the shares that are being transferred are held by a Cambodian taxpayer, then a 20% tax on income (TOI) would apply on any gain derived from the share sale. There currently exists no mechanism under the Cambodian tax regime to subject the transfer of shares in a Cambodian entity by a non-resident shareholder to a capital gains tax or TOI. Recently, the Cambodian tax authority has tried to re-assess gains derived by a non-resident shareholder that has transferred its shareholding in a Cambodian entity. Currently, the issue regarding the application of capital gains tax on the transfer of shares in a Cambodian entity by a non-resident shareholder is being discussed between the private sector in Cambodia and the Cambodian authorities.

There is also a stamp duty of 0.1% that applies to the "market value" of the shares that are transferred in a Cambodian entity—the liable person being the purchaser of the shares and, in practice, the underlying Cambodian entity acting as a proxy for the new shareholder, to pay the stamp tax on its behalf within ninety days of the share transfer being completed. For the purpose of determining the "market value" of shares, the tax authorities will use the higher value of the par value of the shares being transferred, the consideration paid under the share purchase agreement or the net asset value of the company in which the shares are being transferred.

Under Prakas 372, which came into effect in April 2019, the direct transfer of shares by a non-resident shareholder in a Cambodian entity that has retained earnings, or shares that have arisen from an earlier conversion of retained earnings, may trigger a deemed dividend distribution for withholding tax (WHT) purposes.

(iii) Merger by a statutory procedure

The formalities for a statutory merger are set out in the LCE.

Upon receipt of an application to approve a merger, the MOC will issue a certificate of merger. On the date shown in a certificate of merger: (a) the merger of the constituent companies and their continuance as one company becomes effective; (b) the property of each constituent company continues to be the property of the surviving company; (c) the surviving company continues to be liable for the obligations of each constituent company; (d) any civil, criminal or administrative matters involving any constituent company remain effective in relation to the surviving company; and (e) the articles of merger are deemed to be the AOIs of the surviving company and the certificate of merger is deemed to be the certificate of incorporation of the surviving company.

Where the business in the acquired company is a regulated business, approval of the relevant authorities concerned will be required.

Where the business or assets of a QIP company are being transferred, consent or approval from the CDC will be required.

2.12 Relevant Regulatory Authorities

[56] Below are the main governmental authorities that could be relevant to an acquisition in Cambodia.

2.13 CDC

[57] The CDC is the authority responsible for rehabilitation, development and investment activities in Cambodia. The acquisition and merger of companies registered with the CDC and which have been granted QIP status are subject to specific rules pursuant to Sub-Decree 111 on the Implementation of the Amendment to the Law on Investment dated September 27, 2005 (Sub-Decree 111). The Royal Government of Cambodia (RGC) and the National Assembly promulgated the long-awaited new Law on Investment (New Investment Law) on October 15, 2021 to provide a comprehensive, transparent, preferable and predictable legal framework to attract both domestic and foreign investment. The New Investment Law replaces the existing Investment Law. However, according to the New Investment Law, Sub-Decree 111 shall remain in force and effective until it is replaced by a new regulation.

[58] In the event of the merger or acquisition of an investment company holding a QIP, or transfer of the shares in such a company, written approval of the CDC or Provincial/Municipal Investment Sub-Committee (PMIS) is required so that the new entity, buyer or existing QIP holder continues to be entitled to the investment incentives and guarantees. The requirement to obtain approval from the CDC/PMIS for the sale, purchase or merger of a QIP is also stated under the New Investment Law and the detailed process will be stated in a separate Sub-Decree to be adopted by the RGC.

[59] A written request for such approval must be submitted to the CDC or PMIS within ten working days prior to the merger, acquisition or share transfer. The CDC or PMIS will provide its written approval or refusal within ten working days following its receipt of such a request.

[60] If two or more investors, or an investor and any other person, agree to merge to form a new entity, and the new entity wishes to carry out the investor's QIP and be entitled to the investment incentives and guarantees specified in the QIP's registration certificate (RC), the new entity must apply in writing to the CDC or PMIS to be registered as an investor and for the QIP's RC to be transferred to the new entity within ten working days prior to the merger and transfer of the RC.

[61] The CDC or the PMIS must consider the application made and must provide the new entity with written approval or refusal of the registration and the transfer of the RC within ten working days following its receipt of the application.

[62] In the event of failure to apply to the CDC or the PMIS for approval of transfer of shares of a company which has a QIP, as discussed above, the transferee will not be entitled to any of the QIP's investment incentives and guarantees.

2.14 MOC

[63] The MOC is responsible for regulating and promoting trade and commerce in Cambodia. Local and foreign companies which desire to be established in Cambodia must undertake the company registration process using the MOC's online platform, which was launched in early 2016.

[64] Any change of shareholders of a company incorporated in Cambodia is subject to regulatory approval from the MOC. The key approval documents to be issued by the MOC are the approvals (issued via email), the company extract reflecting the relevant changes and the amended AOIs of the company.

2.15 NBC

[65] The NBC is the central bank and is charged with supervising and regulating financial institutions in Cambodia. It has the power to license banks and other financial institutions, regulate money transfers, oversee payment systems, provide credit, conduct foreign exchange transactions, and deal in precious minerals and commodities. NBC's authority to supervise and regulate banks includes authority over micro-finance institutions (MFIs), specialized banks and commercial banks (known collectively as "covered entities"). The NBC's powers also extend to insolvency actions involving covered entities. In addition, the NBC has the power to manage and approve acquisitions of covered entities.

[66] The Law on Banking and Financial Institutions dated November 18, 1999 (Banking Law) contains a number of provisions relating to the acquisition or sale of shares in or by a covered entity. For example, pursuant to Article 23 of the Banking Law, any shareholder, or any group of shareholders acting in concert, shall directly or through the concerned covered entity, notify the NBC of any increase in or transfer of direct or indirect equity holdings in a covered entity which would enable the shareholder or group of shareholders to acquire or to lose 5% of the covered entity's capital or voting rights. However, in practice, any change of shareholding requires the approval of the NBC.

[67] Further, the Banking Law contains a number of provisions restricting the equity interest that may be held by covered entities in other companies.

2.16 Ministry of Economy and Finance

[68] The Ministry of Economy and Finance (MEF) participates in the organization, implementation, and monitoring of the performance of economic and financial policies of the Royal Government of Cambodia. The MEF administers and coordinates the structural reform of the economic and financial institutions and participates in developing, administering and controlling industrial and financial

activities, including bonds, lotto games, lotteries, casinos, retirement funds and other financial reserves.

[69] The Law on Insurance dated August 4, 2014 (Insurance Law) and related regulations regulate the insurance sector in Cambodia. According to the relevant regulations, any change in shareholders of a licensed insurance company must be approved by the Insurance Regulator of Cambodia (IRC). Further, if a licensed insurance company intends to appoint or change the chairman of its board of directors or any director, the licensed insurance company must report the qualifications of the proposed new appointee to the IRC for its examination and approval for such proposed appointment or change.

2.17 Telecommunications Regulator of Cambodia and MPTC

[70] Cambodia's telecommunications industry is primarily regulated by the Law on Telecommunications of Cambodia dated December 17, 2015 (Telecom Law), which addresses such issues as management competence and use of infrastructure and networks, quality standards of service and telecommunications equipment, universal access, national telecommunications numbering plan and electronic addresses, rules on telecommunications service pricing and rights of telecommunications operators, persons related to the telecommunications sector and users.

[71] The Telecommunications Regulator of Cambodia (TRC) was established under Sub Decree 45 dated March 16, 2016, and has autonomy in administrative and regulatory matters as well as having independence from telecommunications operators and persons in relation to the telecommunications sector. Only those persons and entities properly authorized, by way of permission letter, certificate or license, by the TRC, may engage in telecommunications operator services.

[72] The MPTC is responsible for networks and infrastructure supporting the telecommunications sector.

[73] The merger or acquisition of a telecommunications company requires a no-objection letter or an in-principle approval from the TRC. Article 63 of the Telecom Law provides that the TRC shall issue prior approval for a merger or acquisition by shares of a telecommunications operator after receiving the request from the telecommunications operator and subject to other conditions determined by the MPTC. Furthermore, any merger or acquisition is invalid if they have not obtained approval from TRC.

2.18 Electricity Authority of Cambodia

[74] The Ministry of Mines and Energy (MME) (formerly the Ministry of Industry, Mining and Energy) is responsible for the regulation of the generation and provision of electricity in Cambodia. The Electricity Authority of Cambodia (EAC) was established under the Electricity Law dated February 2, 2001 as amended on June 24, 2007 (Electricity Law) as an autonomous regulator to monitor and regulate the power sector in Cambodia. The EAC is responsible for the regulation of both private and public electricity suppliers. For a power project, the EAC is responsible for issuing electricity licenses to relevant project companies.

[75] The Electricity Law governs the electricity sector in Cambodia. Licenses may be issued under the said law in relation to the generation, supply and sale of electricity. Pursuant to Article 29 of the Electricity Law, there are a number of electricity licenses issued by the EAC, including: (i) generation license; (ii) transmission license; (iii) distribution license; (iv) consolidated license; (v) wholesale license; (vi) retail sale license; and (vii) sub-contract license.

[76] The Electricity Law contains a number of provisions that are relevant to the acquisition or sale of shares in a power company. For example, no person, other than the government or a wholly State-owned company, that directly or indirectly owns or controls a licensee may, without the approval of the EAC, own any shares in or have a direct financial interest in any other licensee. Further, under Article 45 of the Electricity Law, the EAC may approve or disapprove a business merger or reorganization, or a major acquisition or sale of assets or securities, by a licensee.

2.19 Controls/Restrictions on Foreign Investment

2.19.1 Restricted Investment Sectors

[77] Cambodia has adopted an open and liberal foreign investment regime. In general, all business activities in Cambodia are permitted, as long as the scope of the investment does not fall under the list of ineligible investment activities, or below the minimum investment capital thresholds, as prescribed in the "Negative List" to be determined by Sub-Decree. Given that the RGC has not issued an implementing Sub-Decree to determine a new "Negative List" for the New Investment Law, the existing "Negative List" as set out under Sub-Decree 111 of the Amendment to the Law on Investment of Cambodia enacted on September 27, 2005 (*Sub-Decree 111*), which is an implementing regulation for the former investment law, remains valid pursuant to Article 38 of the New Investment Law. As such, the "Negative List" of Annex I of Sub-Decree 111 contains prohibitions on investment on grounds of national security, social safety and/or protection of the national economy. Investment in certain highly "sensitive" sectors is prohibited to both national and foreign investors, such as:

(i) production or processing of psychotropic and narcotic substances;
(ii) production of poisonous chemicals, agriculture pesticide/insecticide and other goods by using chemical substances, prohibited by international regulations or the World Health Organization, that affect public health and the environment;
(iii) production and processing of electric power using any waste imported from a foreign count;

(iv) the forestry exploitation businesses; and
(v) other investment activities prohibited by law.

[78] Other forms of investment, as stated in section 2 of the Negative List, are permitted but are ineligible for investment incentives, except for certain activities that meet minimum investment capital thresholds.

[79] Certain other sectors including cigarette manufacturing, alcohol production, movie production, gems, publishing, printing, radio and television, land ownership, pawn shops and pharmaceutical imports and exports require some equity participation or investment by a Cambodian national or require special approvals from government entities for foreign involvement.

[80] Industry-specific licenses are required in certain sectors such as banking, insurance, MFIs, education, transportation, energy, mining, agriculture and telecommunications.

2.20 Restrictions on Foreign Shareholdings

[81] Cambodia places very few restrictions on the level of foreign participation in investments. As a result, a large proportion of foreign investors choose to establish 100% foreign-owned limited companies. However, it should be noted that only a Cambodian company or a Cambodian national can own land.

2.21 Trade Permit (Import and Export Approvals)

[82] In general, both Cambodian and foreign companies are permitted to freely import and export goods in Cambodia. In most cases, no license is required to import goods into Cambodia. Similarly, no export license or permission is required for the exportation of goods out of Cambodia to other countries, except for imports or exports that are subject to prohibition.

[83] A list of prohibited and restricted imports or exports is provided in Sub-Decree 209 on the Enforcement of the List of Prohibited and Restricted Goods dated December 31, 2007 (Sub-Decree 209). Pursuant to Sub-Decree 209, imports or exports are prohibited or restricted, as the case may be, on the following grounds:

(i) protection of national security;
(ii) protection of public order and standards of decency and morality;
(iii) protection of human, animal, or plant life or health;
(iv) protection of national treasures of artistic, historical and/or archeological value;
(v) conservation of natural resources;
(vi) compliance with the prevailing laws of Cambodia; and
(vii) fulfillment of obligations under the Charter of the United Nations.

[84] Importation of raw materials or leather or exportation of furniture or textiles is permitted on the condition that the relevant license or authorization required for import or export, as the case may be, is approved by the relevant authority.

[85] The List of Prohibited and Restricted Goods, as listed in Sub-Decree 209, was updated by the MEF by Letter 3784 dated June 19, 2012, in order to be in alignment with ASEAN Harmonized Tariff Nomenclature (AHTN 2012), with the entirety of the related provisions in Sub-Decree 209 remaining intact.

2.22 Minimum Capital Requirements

[86] Since the introduction of the LALCE, there is no explicit minimum initial capital requirement. As such, the minimum initial required capital for a limited liability company will be that of the combined par value of each share issued. Similarly, since the introduction of the LALCE, there is no explicit minimum par value for shares issues. There are exceptions in certain sectors such as insurance, banking, MFIs and securities companies or if investment incentives are sought, in which case minimum capital requirements may apply.

2.23 Restrictions on Use of Land

[87] A foreign national (either a natural person or a legal entity) is not allowed to own land in Cambodia. As a result, for a foreign investor to purchase land in Cambodia, it is often necessary to set up a trust and/or a joint venture company in which the foreign investor owns 49% of the voting shares, and a Cambodian citizen(s) or Cambodian entity(ies) owns the remaining 51% of the voting shares. A Cambodian entity is defined as having: (1) at least 51% of the voting shares in the company held by a person with Cambodian nationality (either natural or a legal person), as provided under the company's article of incorporation as registered with the MOC; and (2) a place of business and a registered office in Cambodia. Alternatively, a land holding structure may be carried out in the form of a trust arrangement in accordance with Trust Law. For a trust arrangement to be legally valid and enforceable under the Trust Law, a trustee must register the trust with the Trust Regulator within three (3) months following issuance of a permit to create a trust by the Trust Regulator. A trust comes into effect from the issuance date of the trust registration. As the Trust Law and its implementing regulations have only recently been introduced, we are not aware of judicial precedents in which the enforceability of the use of a trust vehicle (where the trustor and/or beneficiary is a foreign national) has been tested.

[88] However, land concessions and long-term leases are permitted for all investors. Presently, under the Civil Code, long-term leases (legally known as perpetual leases) have a minimum duration of fifteen years and a maximum duration of fifty years (and are renewable). A long-term lease right is a right in rem and can be registered on the landowner's certificate of title for the land with the Land Office who will issue a long-term lease certificate upon registration. Long-term leases can only be held up against third parties if they are registered. Short-term leases have a duration of less than fifteen years and cannot be registered at the Land Office. A land concession (economic land concession) is a means of providing state private land through a certain contract to a concessionaire in order to pursue agricultural and agro-industrial activities. The term of an economic land concession must not exceed 50 years and the size must not exceed 10,000 hectares. A person may receive a land concession spread over various locations, however, the total combined area must not exceed 10,000 hectares. It is prohibited to grant economic land concessions covering various locations with a total area exceeding the aforementioned maximum to various individuals and/or legal entities which are under the control of the same individual or entity.

[89] During the concession or lease period, investors may, subject to the terms of each specific concession or lease agreement, mortgage or sub-lease any movable or immovable properties on the land. The transfer or mortgage of concession land, not being used for the purposes under which the concession was granted, is prohibited. The concessionaire shall not be granted ownership rights over land which is subject to an economic land concession. The economic land concession may be subject to succession for its remaining term.

2.24 Use of Foreign Labor

[90] Investors are only allowed to employ foreign employees whose qualifications, skills and expertise are not available among Cambodian citizens. To employ foreign employees, the investors must obtain approval on foreign employee quota from the Ministry of Labor and Vocational Training (MLVT) by November 30 of each year, to employ such foreign employees the following year, following which investors must submit applications for work permits for their foreign employees.

[91] Under the quota system, a maximum of 10% of an employer's local workforce may be foreign nationals (based on a calculation of foreign employees/local employees), including office employees (3%), skilled labor employees (6%) and unskilled labor employees (1%). This quota may be increased (subject to the MLVT's approval) if the enterprise requires employees with specific skills which are currently unavailable in Cambodia.

2.25 Incentives for Foreign Investment

2.25.1 Overview

[92] CDC is the main authority for the government on all strategic and regulatory aspects of QIPs and the development of Special Economic Zones (SEZs) in Cambodia.

Investment incentives are available for QIPs, regardless of whether an investment is from foreign or local investors. Notably, investors who are granted QIP status will be entitled to various incentives. To be entitled to these, QIPs must undergo an investment application and registration process with the CDC or PMIS where the investment project will be located, depending on the type of project and the amount of investment capital. The Sub-Decree on the Establishment of the Sub-Committee on Investment of the Province-Municipalities of the Kingdom of Cambodia was issued in February 2005 to regulate the existing licensing schemes for projects with investment capital of less than USD2 million. The aforementioned sub-decree provides that projects with investment capital under USD2 million must register with the PMIS and those projects with investment capital of USD2 million or greater must register with the CDC in Phnom Penh.

[93] The CDC is responsible for the evaluation and decision-making on all rehabilitation, development and investment project activities. An investor may register a company as an LLC with the MOC and, thereafter, convert this LLC into an investment company (with QIP status) by submitting the relevant application to the CDC. Alternatively, since prior registration with the MOC is not mandatory, establishment of an investment company and registration of the QIP with the CDC can proceed from the outset. Please note that, under the New Investment Law, the registration of an investment project will be done through an online platform. The timeline for granting approval is shortened from the current 31 working day timeline to only 20 working days. Under the New Investment Law, the CDC no longer issues a CRC and FRC and will issue only issue a single registration certificate, which contains a machine-readable bar/QR code.

[94] In addition, the government has improved investment facilitation agencies. For instance, in 2005, the government established the Cambodian Special Economic Zones Board (CSEZB) under the auspices of the CDC to promote the SEZ scheme. Administered by the CSEZB, the Special Economic Zones Administration (SEZA) has established authorized SEZs and provides a one-stop service to investors from the registration of investment projects to obtaining routine export-import approvals.

[95] In keeping with the country's continued efforts to attract investment, in March 2015, the Cambodia Industrial Development Policy (IDP) 2015—2025 was adopted and was officially launched on August 26, 2015. The IDP sets out key policy measures and action plans for two main objectives, which are the promotion of investment and the development of SEZs. To achieve these aims, the CDC is mandated to carry out policy reforms, including amendments to current investment laws and regulations and the adoption of a new law on SEZs.

[96] Policymaking and the New Investment Law will be geared towards: reviewing the criteria for selecting QIPs; the promotion of a favorable investment environment; providing investment incentives and guarantees for investment projects that contribute to skills training, research and development, and innovation; nurturing the growth of Small to Medium-sized Enterprises (*SMEs*); providing more specified investment incentives to the investors; and the reinforcement of institutional capacity, amongst other things.

[97] The new law on SEZs will be developed with a view towards continuing the development of SEZs in provinces, the promotion of hubs for small and medium-sized enterprises (SMEs), the development of industrial corridors and the encouragement of competition among SEZs.

2.26 Investment Incentives

[98] The New Investment Law provides a more comprehensive package of investment incentives than its predecessor. Under the New Investment Law, a QIP entity is still able to choose between a corporate tax exemption period or a special depreciation rate. Under the former, a QIP entity would benefit from a corporate tax exemption ranging from 3 years to 9 years with the added benefit that distributed profits made during the exemption period are not subject to a claw back of corporate tax (which was one of the recognized flaws of the previous Investment Law).

[99] The New Investment Law provides that at the conclusion of the corporate tax exemption period, a QIP entity will be entitled to a graduated corporate rate for an additional six years, i.e., 5% (year 1 & 2), 10% (year 3 & 4) and 15% (year 5 & 6). After year six, the QIP entity would be subject to the standard corporate tax rate of 20% on its taxable profits. QIPs will also receive an exemption from the annual 1% Minimum (turnover) Tax provided they can evidence annual independent audited financial statements.

If a QIP entity elects to use the special depreciation rate, it will be able to apply a 40% tax depreciation rate from the first year that it records fixed assets. In addition to the special depreciation rate, a QIP entity would be eligible to expense certain costs at the rate of 200% for up to nine years.

General Incentives

[100] Under the New Investment Law QIP entities may be eligible for the following additional incentives:

(a) an Export QIP will be eligible for customs duty, excise tax and value-added tax exemption with respect to the importation of construction materials, construction equipment, production equipment and production inputs;
(b) all QIP entities will be eligible for a VAT exemption for the purchase of locally owned production inputs used for the implementation of the QIP; and
(c) all QIP entities will receive a 150% deduction for any of the following expenses:
    (i) research, development, and innovation.
    (ii) human resource development through the provision of vocational training and skills to Cambodian workers/employees.
    (iii) construction of accommodation, canteens, nurseries, and other facilities for workers/employees.
    (iv) upgrading of machinery to serve the production line; and

(v) providing welfare for Cambodian workers/employees, such as comfortable means of transportation for workers/employees to travel from their accommodation to the factory.

Finally—in addition to the incentives set out above, any specific sector and investment activity that has a high potential to contribute to national economic development in Cambodia may receive other special incentives that will be set out in the annual Law on Financial Management.

2.27 Specific Issues of Company/Securities Law

2.27.1 Shareholder Approval

[101] Under the LCE, the directors of any company are required to obtain approval from the shareholders for the sale of all or a major part of the company's assets. In that respect, the directors must first approve the proposed sale themselves before proposing the same to the shareholders.

[102] The AOIs of a company provide specific details of how the approval process is exercised. Generally, under the LCE, a shareholder meeting is required, or a resolution in lieu of a meeting may be provided. While the quorum for a shareholder's meeting can be adjusted pursuant to the AOIs, generally, the quorum for a meeting will be the holders of 51% of the shares. Approval of transactions is by way of ordinary majority unless the AOIs or shareholders agreement state otherwise.

2.28 Directors' Duties

[103] Directors' duties under the LCE are fairly general. The LCE provides a requirement to (i) act in the best interests of the company and honestly and in good faith; and (ii) exercise the care, diligence and skill that a reasonably prudent person would exercise in comparable circumstances. These terms, however, are not defined in the LCE, and there is no guidance as to how such duties apply in an M&A transaction. There are no specific considerations that arise in the event of hostile transactions, other than the broad application of the requirements referred to above.

[104] Under Article 134 of the LCE, a director must disclose the nature and extent of his/her interest in writing to the company if he/she:

(i) is a party to a contract or a proposed contract with the company; or
(ii) has a material interest in any person who is a party to a contract or a proposed contract with the company.

[105] Further, under Article 137 of the LCE, a director who has a conflict of interest is not allowed to vote on any resolution to approve the contract unless the contract is:

(i) an arrangement by way of security for money lent to or obligations undertaken by him/her for the benefit of the company or an affiliate;
(ii) one relating primarily to his/her remuneration as a director, officer, employee or agent of the company or an affiliate;
(iii) one for indemnity or insurance; or
(iv) one with an affiliate.

[106] Pursuant to Article 140 of the LCE, a director who votes for or consents to a resolution authorizing the issuance of shares for consideration other than money is jointly and severally liable to the company for the amount by which the consideration received is less than the fair amount the company would have received if the shares had been issued for money. However, a director must not be held liable if he or she proves that they did not know and could not reasonably have known that the shares were issued for a consideration less than the fair value. The action to enforce such liability must be taken within two years following the date of the resolution which approved the issuance of shares.

[107] Moreover, according to Article 141 of the LCE, a director who votes for or consents to a resolution authorizing a purchase, redemption or another acquisition of shares, a reduction of stated capital, or a payment of a dividend contrary to the requirements of the law is jointly and severally liable to restore to the company any amounts so distributed or paid.

[108] It should be noted that the LCE does not provide the method for calculating the value of contributions other than money and, therefore, it is the duty of the directors to make sure that their decisions meet the requirements of the LCE.

[109] Directors' duties are able to be enforced through arbitration between shareholders and directors if the AOIs so provide; otherwise, the LCE provides for derivative actions to be brought by shareholders on behalf of the company.

2.29 Form of Consideration

[110] Pursuant to Article 146 of the LCE, payment for shares may be cash and non-cash consideration, including past services. Payment in kind may be made, and this includes rights to use intellectual and intangible property.

[111] The process for valuation of any payment is determined by the directors whose decision is final in the absence of any fraud. As Cambodian law requires shares to be paid up prior to issue, once the value of consideration is accepted, there are no restrictions on subsequent disposals, unless the AOIs or shareholders agreement state otherwise.

2.30 Financial Assistance

[112] Cambodian law does not contain any specific provisions regarding financial assistance by a company for the purchase of its own shares.

2.31 Security Interests

[113] Cambodian law allows for a range of security interests to be taken under two operative pieces of legislation, namely (i) the Civil Code (2007); and (ii) the Law on Secured Transactions (2007) (LST).

[114] For moveable assets, the main forms of security interest are a pledge, being a possessory security interest or a security interest granted under the LST.

[115] The LST is not concerned with nomenclature, so security interests can be called whatever is agreed between the parties, i.e., a charge, security interest, pledge, or assignment by way of security. Provided there is a written agreement, and the agreement grants a right to certain collateral to secure the performance of an obligation.

[116] The LST does not deal with concepts of "fixed" and "floating" but, similar to other jurisdictions using a personal property security law, it does deal with attachment and perfection. The perfection of the interest, through possession or registration, grants the holder of the perfected interest with priority to the collateral being granted as security. The collateral being offered as security is simply defined by the security agreement itself.

[117] Registration of security interests under the LST occurs through a centralized online platform operated by the Secured Transactions Filing Office of the MOC. Registration is deemed to be public notification of the perfected security interest.

[118] While the holder of the perfected security interest has rights to possession of the secured property in the event of default pursuant to the LCE, in practice, this will still require the assistance of a court in situations where the debtor is not willing to give up possession of the secured property.

[119] In situations of insolvency, pursuant to Article 57 of the Law on Insolvency, proceeds from the liquidation of any company are subject to the following order of priority:

- (i) wages of employees, remuneration for provisional administrator, administrative fees and court fees;
- (ii) secured claims up to the higher of the value of the secured portion of the claim as determined by the provisional administrator or the net proceeds from an effective sale of the encumbered asset (collateral);
- (iii) state taxes which have not been filed; and
- (iv) admissible unsecured claims and the amount of secured claims exceeding the limit specified in subparagraph (ii).

[120] In addition, once an insolvency proceeding under the Law on Insolvency has commenced, no action, proceeding or execution process may be commenced or continued against the debtor or the estate of the debtor, except that the administrator may authorize the secured creditors in writing to repossess and sell the debtor's encumbered assets in accordance with applicable law or in any other way avail themselves of their security right and obtain repayment by separate individual action. Further, once such insolvency has commenced, any valuation of any security rights against the assets of a debtor must be undertaken by the administrator.

[121] For security over immovable property, the primary security is the hypothec, being a non-possessory form of a mortgage. Registration of a hypothec over immovable property is completed in the specific land office where the land is situated, and there is currently no single centralized registry for filing of immovable property security interests. The filing process is document-intensive and strictly followed.

[122] Enforcement of immovable property security can only be achieved through Court order.

2.32 Completion Formalities

[123] Transfers of shares, land and assets all involve different levels of formality and complexity in Cambodia.

[124] For shares, registration of any transfer must be made with the relevant authorities (including the MOC), and a comprehensive list of documents is required to be provided to effect the transfer. For share transfers, most documents are required to be signed by the respective seller, buyer and target in accordance with the formality requirements of the MOC.

[125] For asset transfers, these will depend on the nature of the assets. Usually, an asset transfer will simply be effected by way of the operative agreement between the buyer and seller. Motor vehicles, for example, may require ownership transfer papers to be registered with the relevant transport ministry.

[126] For land transfers, this requires a comprehensive list of documentation and notarization of the operative documents and must be effected by registration with the Ministry of Land Management, Urban Planning and Construction.

2.33 Costs and Fees

[127] Aside from professional fees, the costs for share transfers include the filing fees for updated AOIs filed with the MOC, and a stamp tax of 0.1% levied by the GDT, which is levied on the higher of the par value of the shares, the net asset value of the target company or the transfer price of the shares as described in the transaction documents.

[128] Other costs will depend on the nature of the target entity. Banks, for example, have additional costs with respect to the requirements of the NBC.

2.34 Dividends

[129] Dividends of a company may only be issued out of surpluses or net profits as provided by Article 157 of the LCE. Subject to the AOIs of the company, there are no reserve requirements prescribed by law and no restrictions on distributions to domestic or foreign shareholders.

2.35 Purchase of Own Shares

[130] Under Article 155 of the LCE, subject to its AOIs, a company is (theoretically) entitled to purchase or redeem its own shares. However, a company may not purchase or redeem shares if there are reasonable grounds to believe that the company will not be able to pay its liabilities on the due date and that the realizable value of the company's assets would be less than the aggregate of its liabilities.

2.36 Corporate Veil

[131] Article 284 of the LCE states that a subsidiary company has a legal personality separate from its principals. Article 147 of the LCE limits the liability of a shareholder of a company to the price of the shareholder's subscription. Unless the parent company of a Cambodian registered subsidiary has contractually agreed to be liable for the debts or liabilities of its subsidiary, the parent company will be afforded the same legal rights as all other shareholders of limited liability companies in Cambodia, namely the right to have its liability limited to the price of its share subscription.

[132] For the sake of completeness, it is noted that influential shareholders of registered banks and financial institutions ("influential" being a shareholder holding 20% or more of the voting rights) are required by the NBC to agree to provide financial support to the bank or financial institution in circumstances where the bank or financial institution falls below certain solvency levels.

2.37 Insolvency

[133] Acquisition of shares, or buying businesses that have gone into insolvency requires the approval of the administrator appointed to manage the insolvency. Upon insolvency, the company and its shares are effectively frozen, and all dealings must be approved by the administrator and the court.

2.38 Choice of Law

[134] Although the choice of foreign law as governing law for a contract is legal, valid and binding under Cambodian laws and is specifically recognized in the Commercial Arbitration Law promulgated on May 5, 2006, and although Cambodian laws do not impose any restriction on the choice of governing law, current judicial practice indicates that the courts of Cambodia may not be willing or be able to recognize or give effect to the laws of any jurisdiction other than Cambodia given its lack of expertise in some areas of substantive laws and the potential differences between civil and common law regimes.

[135] While there is no restriction preventing the parties from submitting to the jurisdiction of a foreign court, the Cambodian Code of Civil Procedures specifies that a final judgment of a foreign court is deemed valid and may be enforced by Cambodian courts without examining the merits of the matter unless:

(i) the foreign court did not have jurisdiction to hear the matter;
(ii) the foreign court judgment was issued by default (i.e., ex parte);
(iii) the foreign court judgment violates the public policy of Cambodia;
(iv) there is no reciprocity of enforcement of judgments between Cambodia and the country in which the foreign court is based; and
(v) the foreign court judgment is not final and conclusive.

[136] There is, to our knowledge, no law or treaty conferring jurisdiction on any foreign court nor any guarantee of reciprocity between Cambodia and any foreign country, other than Vietnam. Accordingly, based on the criteria set out in the Code of Civil Procedures as set out above, in our view, it is unlikely that any foreign court judgment will be enforced by Cambodian courts.

[137] While, theoretically, a Cambodian court may legally be able to apply foreign law, as a practical matter, the Cambodian courts will likely have no way of applying foreign laws as they have no practical understanding of such substantive foreign laws and simply would not be able to enforce foreign laws if the relevant contract was ever litigated in a Cambodian court.

[138] Cambodia is a party to the 1958 New York Convention on the Recognition and Enforcement of Foreign Arbitral Awards (New York Convention) and has enacted the Law on Commercial Arbitration and the Code of Civil Procedures, which read together, require that foreign arbitral awards be recognized, upheld and enforced by the courts of Cambodia without re-trying the case or otherwise examining the merits, except in certain circumstances.

[139] On the domestic front, in 2010, the government provided for the establishment of the National Commercial Arbitration Center (NCAC), Cambodia's first alternative dispute resolution mechanism, to enable investors to resolve commercial disputes more quickly and inexpensively than through the court system. The NCAC was officially launched in March 2013 and is composed of independently elected members, who have been selected and trained in arbitration at the Singapore International Arbitration Center and the Singapore Institute of Arbitrators.

[140] Accordingly, submission to NCAC or foreign arbitration is both common and recommended in Cambodian M&A transactions.

[141] Please refer to paragraphs [201]–[209] and [210]–[213] for more details on NCAC and foreign arbitration and enforcement, respectively.

2.39 Specific Rules on Public Takeovers

[142] As of the date of this publication, public takeovers must be disclosed to and subject to a prior approval of the Securities and Exchange Regulator of Cambodia (SERC). Apart from this general requirement under the corporate disclosure regulation, a draft regulation is being prepared to set out the detailed rules on public takeovers of a public listed company, although the draft has not been made publicly available. While developments are being made and new regulations drafted, Cambodia's securities market still remains relatively nascent with the Law on the Issuance and Trading of Non-Government Securities being promulgated in 2007 and the Cambodian Stock Exchange being established in mid-2011.

[143] There is, however, a restriction on the transfer of shares in a public limited company during the first year of listing. For a period of one year from the official listing date, a shareholder holding a controlling interest (being a shareholder or group of related persons holding the voting shares of at least 30% of the total voting shares, either directly or indirectly) is prohibited from transferring any and all of its shares for the first six months and is only permitted to transfer up to 50% of its shares during the remaining six months.

[144] An acquisition of a controlling interest in a public limited company must first be approved by the SERC and carried out in accordance with any requirements determined by the SERC (in addition to the registration requirements with the MOC as discussed under paragraphs [28]–[30] or regulatory approval from the competent regulator).

[145] Under Article 66 of Sub-Decree 54 on Implementation of the Law on Issuance and Trading of Non-Government Securities, the SERC may make a decision or adopt rules to ensure that:

(i) the acquisition of a controlling interest in a public limited company is undertaken in a fair and transparent manner;
(ii) the identity of a potential purchaser who proposes to acquire the controlling interest in a public limited company is disclosed to the current holders of the voting shares;
(iii) the current holders of the voting shares are given sufficient time to consider the proposed acquisition;
(iv) the current holders of the voting shares are given sufficient information to enable them to assess the merits of the proposed acquisition;
(v) the current holders of relevant classes of voting shares are given reasonable and equal opportunity to enjoy the benefits offered by a potential purchaser

who proposes to acquire a controlling interest in a public limited company; and

(vi) a person who acquires or disposes of a controlling interest in a public limited company must make full and accurate disclosure in respect of such controlling interest.

[146] Based on the above, it seems that there is no prohibition or restriction on the public announcement of a proposed takeover of a controlling interest in a public limited company. Nevertheless, based on our past dealings with Cambodian regulators, Cambodian regulators prefer that a proposed takeover not be publicly announced before the competent regulators consent to or issue approval-in-principle for such proposal.

[147] In the absence of specific laws and regulations, a public takeover of a public limited company would generally be subject to the requirements determined by the SERC.

2.40 Other Relevant Laws

2.40.1 Anti-corruption

Overview of ACL

[148] The primary legal instrument governing anti-corruption in Cambodia is the ACL, which came into force on April 17, 2010, as amended on August 1, 2011. The ACL created an Anti-Corruption Institution composed of the National Council for Anti-Corruption and the Anti-Corruption Unit (ACU), which replaced the previous Anti-Corruption Body.

[149] Under the supervision of the National Council for Anti-Corruption, the ACU has significant judicial police powers to investigate instances of alleged corruption, as well as to propose measures related to corrupt practices in ministries, institutions, public and private units.

[150] Under the ACL, all corruption offenses defined in the Criminal Code dated November 30, 2009 (Criminal Code) are to be implemented as part of the ACL.

Bribery/Corruption Offense under the ACL

[151] Corruption offenses, as defined in the ACL and Criminal Code, include a wide range of offenses.

[152] Article 605 of the Criminal Code states:

> shall be penalized from 5 to 10-year imprisonment, any person who, without being entitled to, directly or indirectly provides a donation or gift, makes a promise or provides any benefit to a public official or a citizen entrusted with a public mandate through election in order that such public official or elected public official: (i) performs any acts of his/her functions or facilitates any acts

by using his/her functions; or (ii) refrains from performing his/her duties or facilitating any acts by using his/her functions.

[153] Article 605 of the Criminal Code applies where the recipient of the benefit performs any acts of his/her functions or refrains from performing any such act as a result of receiving a donation, gift, promise or benefit.

[154] While Article 605 of the Criminal Code does not explicitly prohibit unofficial payments made to officials for routine non-discretionary services, officials of the ACU have indicated publicly that such payments are prohibited under Cambodian law. On this basis, it is now commonly understood in the business community that facilitation payments are prohibited in Cambodia under the ACL.

2.40.2 Anti-money Laundering

[155] The AMLCTF, adopted on June 27, 2020, is the main legislation in relation to Anti-Money Laundering (AML) and terrorism financing that is, generally, applicable to money laundering prevention and enforcement in Cambodia. The AMLCTF replaces the Law on Anti-Money Laundering and Combating the Financing of Terrorism dated June 24, 2007, as amended on June 3, 2013. However, existing implementing regulations under the previous law continue to apply to the extent not amended by the AMLCTF and/or the newer implementing regulations.

[156] AMLCTF provides the legal framework for money laundering and terrorism financing prevention in Cambodia. Reporting entities broadly include banks, financial services institutions, money exchange and remittance services, investment companies, investment funds, trusts, dealers of precious metals and stones, real estate companies, casinos, non-governmental organizations and professional service firms. Professional service firms such as lawyers, notaries, accountants, auditors, investment advisors and asset managers are considered reporting entities under the AMLCTF when they prepare for and carry out transactions for their clients relating to the following business activities:

(i) buying and selling real estate;
(ii) managing client money, securities or other assets including managing bank accounts and organizing contributions of company capital;
(iii) forming legal entities for the purpose of buying or selling other entities; or
(iv) acting in trust or as a company preparing for or carrying out transactions for a client, specifically (a) acting as a formation agent of legal persons; (b) acting as or arranging for another person to act as a director, partner or similar position for a legal entity, a partner of a partnership or a similar position in relation to other legal persons; (c) providing a registered office; business address or accommodation, correspondence or administrative address for a company, a partnership or any other legal person or arrangement; (d) acting as or arranging for another person to act as a trustee of an express trust, and (e) acting as or arranging another to act as a nominee shareholder for another person.

[157] Some of the most important obligations created by the AMLCTF are:

(i) undertaking risk-based customer due diligence measures by applying enhanced customer due diligence measures (if the customers are in the high-risk category) and normal customer due diligence measures (if the customers are not in the high-risk category);
(ii) reporting entities must develop programs for the prevention of money laundering and financing of terrorism in accordance with the Cambodian Financial Intelligence Unit (CAFIU)'s directive and shall include the following: (a) establish internal policies, procedures, and controls including appropriate compliance arrangements and adequate screening procedures to ensure high standards when hiring employees; (b) appoint a compliance officer at senior management level; (c) ongoing training for officers or employees; and (d) internal audit function to check compliance with and effectiveness of the measures taken to apply under the AMLCTF;
(iii) the compliance officer is responsible for establishing internal policies, developing appropriate procedures and a manual of compliance, and ensuring all employees of the reporting are in compliance with AML regulations, policies, procedures and the manual of compliance;
(iv) maintain records of its customers' identification and transactions for five years after the account has been closed or the business relations with the customers have ended; and
(v) submit cash transactions and report suspicious transactions to the CAFIU.

[158] The CAFIU is the regulator of AML activities and terrorism financing prevention in Cambodia. CAFIU is responsible for analyzing information submitted to it and sending relevant information to law enforcement authorities. The National Coordination Committee on Anti-Money Laundering and Financing of Terrorism and Combating the Financing of Proliferation of Weapons of Mass Destruction (NCC) is the high-level policymaker and coordinator for the implementation of the AMLCTF and the Law on Combating the Financing of Proliferation of Weapon of Mass Destruction dated June 27, 2020. The NCC comprises the ministers of various government ministries, the head of the NBC and CAFIU, and a representative of the National Counter-Terrorism Committee. CAFIU also acts as the secretariat to support the performance of NCC's roles and duties.

[159] The sanctions under the new AMLCTF include disciplinary and criminal sanctions. The disciplinary sanctions include warning, reprimand, prohibition or limitation to conduct any transactions for a period of time determined by the supervisory authorities, revocation of the business license, the proposal to demote relevant officials or directors of the reporting entities and fines. Criminal sanctions include monetary fines and imprisonment. Criminal offenses under the AMLCTF include money laundering, denial of required information, negligence in providing transaction reports, violation of disclosure of information and tipping off, violation of the obligations to keep professional secrecy and terrorism financing with additional penalties for legal entities. The penalties for criminal offenses under the AMLCTF are more severe than the penalty provisions under the previous laws, with fines of up to KHR2 billion (approximately USD500 000).

[160] The Prakas on Anti-Money Laundering and Combating the Financing of Terrorism (May 30, 2008) and the Prakas on Anti-Money Laundering and Combating the Financing of Terrorism Relating to All Reporting Entities Not Regulated by the NBC (December 21, 2010) cover "reporting entities" that are regulated by the NBC (the 2008 Prakas) and those that are not regulated by the NBC (the 2010 Prakas). As mentioned above, these two Prakas remain in effect until being replaced by newer regulations. The two Prakas are substantially similar and clarify the policies and procedures that are required by the AMLCTF. Notably, the two Prakas:

(i) impose specific requirements for conducting business with "politically exposed persons;"
(ii) require reporting entities to have information management systems in place;
(iii) require reporting entities to have a policy manual, that contains the reporting entity's procedures to comply with the law;
(iv) specify the acceptable types of identification and the procedures for identifying individual and corporate customers;
(v) require the company to ensure its corporate customers are not in the process of being dissolved or wound up; and
(vi) prohibit doing business with shell entities that engage in no commercial business of their own regardless of whether the shell entity has the legal capacity to enter into such a transaction.

2.40.3 Product Safety

[161] The Law on the Management of Quality and Safety of Products and Services dated June 26, 2000 (*LMQSPS*) governs the general obligations of manufacturers and services providers to, among other things, indicate on their products, goods and services (in the Khmer language) the ingredients, composition, users' guidelines, manufacturing date and expiration date along with other requirements which guarantee the safety and health of consumers prior to their commercialization. Additionally, there are industry-specific product safety regulations (e.g., the Department of Drugs and Food under the Ministry of Health is responsible for the quality and control of pharmaceuticals and is authorized to conduct inspections at manufacturing plants, drug import/export companies and pharmacies/retail outlets). Further, Cambodia recently enacted the Law on Food Safety, dated June 8, 2022 (*Food Safety Law*), which aims to manage food quality and safety in all stages of the production chain and the food business in Cambodia. The Food Safety Law also applies to imported foods. The Civil Code addresses, generally and briefly, product liability under Articles 751–753, as well as general negligence and intentional acts causing harm under Articles 742–744. Under the above provisions, where an unreasonably dangerous defect exists in a manufactured movable item and harm results to another due to such defect, the manufacturer (which includes an importer and distributor of such manufactured goods) is liable for damages, unless the defect could not have been discovered based on the scientific standards existing at the time of manufacture.

[162] Further, the above provisions provide that any person who owns or manages an automobile or other transportation apparatus, an explosive item, radioactive substance, toxic chemical or other highly dangerous item is liable for damages for any harm caused to another.

2.40.4 Environmental Protection

Environmental Laws

[163] The two main pieces of legislation governing environmental issues are the Law on Environmental Protection and Management of Natural Resources dated December 24, 1996 (Environmental Protection Law) and Sub-Decree 72 on Environmental Impact Assessment dated August 11, 1999 (Sub-Decree 72). The Environmental Protection Law was enacted to protect, promote and restore Cambodia's natural environment and to ensure the conservation, development, management and sustainable use of natural resources. We understand that the Cambodian Government is currently also drafting an Environmental Code.

[164] The Environmental Protection Law empowers the Ministry of Environment (MOE) to inspect any premises or any means of transport if the MOE considers that it affects the environment. To ensure the sustainability of natural resources, the Environmental Protection Law requires all ministries to consult with the MOE before issuing decisions or undertaking activities related to the protection, development or management of the use of natural resources.

[165] The Environmental Protection Law is supported by various governmental regulations including, *inter alia*, the Sub-Decree 72, the Sub-Decree on Water Pollution Control, the Sub-Decree on Solid Waste Management and the Sub-Decree on Control of Air and Noise Pollution.

Environmental Impact Assessments

[166] Article 2 of Sub-Decree 72 outlines the principles that an Environmental Impact Assessment (EIA) is required for certain projects due to their nature, size, or activity. There are two types of EIA: (i) initial environmental impact assessment report (IEIA); and (ii) full environmental impact assessment/environmental and social impact assessment report (Full EIA). A Full EIA is a detailed study on the environmental impact of the project and is required to be conducted when a project is deemed to have a serious impact on the environment and public welfare.

[167] Investors whose projects are subject to an EIA are required to submit the EIA report to the MOE. For projects that may have severe environmental impacts. Full EIA reports must also be submitted to the MOE. The approval of the MOE on the EIA report must be obtained before commencing the project. For clarity, Prakas 21 dated February 3, 2020 on classification of environmental impact assessment for development project detail which types of project fall under the requirement of either IEIA or Full EIA.

In addition to the EIA, the project company of the investors will be required to execute an environmental protection agreement with the MOE (EPA). An EPA contains undertakings to implement the conditions prescribed in the Full EIA and comply with environmental laws and regulations, in particular, those related to waste management and air and noise pollution, biological environment and socio-economic environment and requirement for submission of the environmental monitoring report(s), and to cooperate with the MOE officials for any authorized inspection of the project site.

[168] Furthermore, it is a requirement under an EPA that the project company pays contributions to: (i) the environment endowment fund for environmental protection; and (ii) the environmental and social fund in accordance with Sub-Decree 238 on the establishment of environmental and social endowment fund. Further, the investors are also required to pay a service fee for examining the EIA report.

[169] Prakas 376 dated September 2, 2009 on general guidelines for developing initial and full environmental impact assessment reports sets out the process and guidelines for preparation of the EIA whereby the project owner with its owned qualified professional capacity recognized by MOE may prepare the IEIA or Full EIA and submit to the MOE or may use consulting company registered and recognized by the MOE to prepare the IEIA or Full EIA and submit to MOE.

In principle, it takes at least thirty working days to obtain the approval from the EIA/EPA upon a complete dossier having been successfully submitted to the MOE.

2.40.5 Intellectual Property Rights

Overview

[170] With the accession to the WTO, Cambodia has now introduced a fully developed matrix of intellectual property rights (IPR) regulations.

[171] In this region, investors will find that protection and enforcement of their IPR is an area of their business that merits close attention, particularly with the rapid growth in public awareness of international brands and home-grown enterprises needing to protect their interests both locally and on the global stage. Key developments in this area expected in the near future include a Law on the Protection of Undisclosed Information, a Sub-Decree Implementing Special Border Measures in the Trademark Law and a Sub-Decree Implementing the Copyright Law.

[172] Among the different types of intellectual property, trademark protection (including registration of marks, official recognition of trademark licensing agreements, and enforcement of such rights) is the most developed area, with a relatively robust administrative framework that allows trademark holders and government authorities to enforce these rights. Protection for registered designs and patents are lagging.

Trademarks

[173] In February 2002, the Law Concerning Marks, Trade Names, and Acts of Unfair Competition (Trademark Law) entered into force, although registration of trademarks was possible prior to then. This section sets out the legal regime under this law as well as under related ministerial regulations and practices currently in effect.

[174] The Trademark Law is relatively comprehensive in its scope as it covers, among other things, the protection of trademarks and service marks, when an objection to registration may be made, and the priority given to the applicant when there has been a previous registration in another country. The protection given to trademark owners is also defined, as well as their right to assign, transfer and license their trademarks. Civil remedies, as well as administrative remedies, are made available under the Trademark Law. Key provisions of the Cambodian trademark system under the Trademark Law are discussed below:

(a) Registration procedure and rights conferred by registration
Applications to register a mark are filed with the Department of Intellectual Property of the MOC. The application to the MOC must be accompanied by samples of the mark to be registered, applicant details, specification of the goods and/or services in each class as well the filing fee for each class. The registration process is complete when a certificate of registration is issued to the applicant and is published in the Official Gazette of the MOC. The registration is valid for ten years. An affidavit of use is required to be submitted to the MOC during the fifth year of registration in order to keep the registration valid for the entire ten-year period. Registration can be opposed within ninety days of publication in the Official Gazette. An applicant outside Cambodia must be represented by an agent residing and practising in Cambodia. A registered mark that is not used for a continuous period of five years is subject to cancellation unless the applicant or owner submits an affidavit of use/non-use. A mark can be licensed to a user through the use of a license contract. Such a contract must be filed with the MOC for the license to be enforceable to third parties.

(b) Enforcement
Infringement includes the use of a registered mark in Cambodia by an unauthorized person and the unauthorized use of a sign identical, or confusingly similar, to the registered mark or a well-known mark not registered in Cambodia.
The owner of a registered mark may apply to customs, competent authorities or the court to suspend clearance of goods suspected of being counterfeit by proving ownership of the mark and its unauthorized use by a third party. The Trademark Law authorizes interested persons to consult the register of marks and obtain extracts from it. All registrations, renewals, refusals or removals of the mark are registered and published in the Official Gazette by the MOC.
On October 4, 1996, Cambodia entered into an agreement with the U.S. known as the Agreement on Trade Relations and Intellectual Property Rights Protection. This agreement was ratified in early 1997 by Cambodia's National Assembly. In this agreement, Cambodia agreed, among other things, to become a member of the Berne Convention for the Protection of

Literary and Artistic Works, to protect all works encompassed by that convention and to ensure adequate enforcement measures to protect intellectual property.

Patents

[175] The Law on Patents, Utility Model Certificates and Industrial Designs (Patent Law) was promulgated in January 2003 (and recently amended in 2020 to recognize, in certain circumstances, the protection afforded by registered European patents, utility model certificates, and industrial designs in Cambodia). This law has, as its primary objectives: (a) the encouragement of innovation; (b) scientific and technological research and development; (c) the stimulation and promotion of increased internal and external commerce and investment; (d) the promotion of the transfer of technology to Cambodia in order to facilitate industrial activity and the development of the economy; and (e) the protection of industrial property rights and to combat the infringement thereof from illegal business practices.

[176] A "patent" grants an inventor the right to prevent others from using their "invention" without authorization, while an "invention" is the idea of an inventor that provides a novel, industrially applicable solution to a special problem in the field of technology. A patentable invention is one that:

(a) is new;
(b) involves an inventive step; and
(c) is industrially applicable.

[177] Non-patentable inventions include:

(a) discoveries, scientific theories, and mathematical methods;
(b) schemes, rules, or methods for doing business, performing, purely mental acts, or playing games;
(c) methods (but not products) for treatment of the human or animal body;
(d) certain pharmaceutical products; and
(e) plants and animals.

[178] The inventor is entitled to the right to the patent. However, the Patent Law recognizes the right of the employer, not the inventor, where an invention is made pursuant to the execution of an employment contract.

[179] In order to have a new invention protected, the inventor must file an application for a patent with the Ministry of Industry, Science, Technology and Innovation (MISTI). The MISTI will issue a patent to the applicant following its examination of the application and the required documentation and information. The patent is valid for twenty years, subject to the payment of an annual fee, and can be assigned or licensed.

[180] Cambodia officially joined the Hague Agreement Concerning the International Registration of Industrial Designs on February 25, 2017. The Hague mechanism, administered by the World Intellectual Property Organisation, will allow Cambodian businesses to request IPR protection for their industrial designs with all other member countries through a single application.

Copyright

[181] The Law on Copyright and Related Rights was promulgated on March 5, 2003 (Copyright Law) and aims to help secure the rights of authors with respect to works and to protect the works of authors, performers, phonogram producers and broadcasting organizations to ensure a just and legitimate exploitation of such cultural products.

[182] Copyright in a work exists automatically (i.e., without the need to register the right) so long as the work falls into one of the following categories:

(a) works of authors who are Cambodian nationals or habitual residents;
(b) works first published in Cambodia;
(c) audio-visual works, the producer of which is headquartered in, or is a habitual resident of Cambodia;
(d) works of architecture erected in Cambodia and other artistic works incorporated in a building or other structure located in Cambodia; or
(e) works to which Cambodia is obliged to grant protection under international treaties.

[183] The author of work enjoys an exclusive incorporeal property right in that work, which is enforceable against all persons. This right includes moral rights and economic rights. The moral right of the author is perpetual, cannot be forfeited, cannot be seized to meet an obligation and may not be subject to prescription. However, an author of a copyright work may waive its moral rights, and they may be transmitted upon death to the heirs of the author. Where there is no heir, this right will be subject to the administration and governance of the Ministry of Culture and Fine Arts (MCFA).

[184] Essentially, the moral rights of the author are:

(a) the exclusive right to decide the manner and timing of the disclosure of the work; and
(b) the right to oppose all forms of distortion or modification of the content of the work, which would be prejudicial to the author's honor or reputation.

[185] The protection of economic rights in work commences from the date of creation and generally ends fifty years following the author's death. Economic rights cover the following acts in relation to work:

(a) translation or adaptation;
(b) rental, sale and distribution to the public of the original or a copy;
(c) importation into Cambodia of reproductions; and

(d) public performance, public display, broadcasting or other communication to the public.

[186] Equally important to note are the limitations on the owner's rights, which allow the use of the work in the following instances (among others):

(a) importation for personal use;
(b) use for the purpose of education that is not for financial gain; and
(c) analysis, short quotations and citations.

[187] Contracts, such as license agreements, in relation to the exploitation of economic rights, must be in writing to be valid.

[188] Although works are automatically protected, the owners of copyright works may deposit their works at the MCFA. Upon payment of a registration fee, the MCFA will issue a certificate of registration for the registered work. Please note that registration of a work protected by copyright is voluntary and is not required for enforcement of the right against infringement by a third party.

[189] In addition to the rights of authors, the Copyright Law also protects the rights of performers, phonogram producers, video producers and broadcasting organizations, covering the recording, reproduction, sale, rental and communication to the public of performances, phonograms, videos and broadcasts. In particular, the Copyright Law provides that use of a phonogram recording for broadcasting or public performance entitles the performer and the producer to a single payment from the user.

[190] The duration of protection for the performer is fifty years starting from the end of the calendar year in which the performance was recorded in the phonogram or in the absence of such recording, from the end of the year in which the performance took place.

[191] On October 4, 1996, Cambodia entered into an agreement with the U.S. known as the Agreement on Trade Relations and Intellectual Property Rights Protection. This agreement was ratified in early 1997 by Cambodia's National Assembly. In this agreement, Cambodia agreed, amongst other things, to become a member of the Berne Convention for the Protection of Literary and Artistic Works, to protect all works encompassed by that convention and to ensure adequate enforcement measures to protect copyright in works originating in other member countries as it would to its own nationals.

2.41 Due Diligence Process

[192] Legal due diligence in Cambodia typically focuses on:

(i) the ownership of the target company and the extent of the capital contributed by the shareholders;

(ii) compliance of the target company's constitutional documents with the laws of Cambodia;
(iii) the validity and sufficiency of all regulatory approvals and licenses required for the operation of the target company's business activities, including environmental approvals, permits and licenses, if applicable;
(iv) material contracts to which the target company is a party;
(v) financial indebtedness and security agreements to which the target company is a party;
(vi) main assets owned/leased by the target company;
(vii) intellectual property owned, transferred, licensed or sublicensed by or to the target company;
(viii) Cambodian law issues arising, if any, from the land owned/leased by the target company;
(ix) labor law obligations and compliance issues; and
(x) litigation or other dispute proceedings, actual, pending or threatened, involving the target company.

[193] Further, the following public searches can be undertaken as part of the due diligence process:

(i) an online corporate search on the target company's particulars registered in the automated (online) system of the MOC;
(ii) a secured interests search with the Secured Transactions Filing Office of the MOC to confirm whether any assets of or interests in the target company are encumbered;
(iii) a land title/property search to confirm whether there are any registered liens and encumbrances, foreign ownership restrictions, rights to transfer title, government restrictions, systematic re-titling obligations, potential historical site obligations affecting the use of the property by the target company, disputes and/or zone classifications;
(iv) a trademark search with the Department of Intellectual Property of the MOC to confirm whether each trademark of the target company is duly registered; and
(v) a litigation search limited to the records of the Phnom Penh Court of First Instance and any applicable provincial court for any possible civil and criminal litigation as well as insolvency/bankruptcy cases concerning the Cambodian subsidiary and its directors.

[194] Among the problems likely to be encountered in legal due diligence in Cambodia are:

(i) lack of information due to poor bookkeeping and a general disinclination to disclose information by the target company. The collection of data to conduct comprehensive due diligence can be time-consuming in Cambodia. Cambodian parties may be reluctant to disclose information about the target companies to outsiders, in particular foreigners. Also, more often than not, particular sets of information or documents may simply not be available due to a lack of proper bookkeeping and compliance with Cambodian laws;

(ii) due diligence is a fairly new concept to some Cambodian target companies, so the exercise can take longer and be more burdensome than in other jurisdictions. Though physical data rooms are used on occasion, virtual data rooms are increasingly being used to facilitate the disclosure process. Most of the information and documents disclosed are in the Khmer language;

(iii) publicly available information may be incomplete and unreliable. For example, there is no centralized database of litigation information in Cambodia. As a result, only basic information is available through the search (e.g., names of the parties, number and date of the complaint and brief facts). Also, many security interests are not properly registered, so it is difficult to ascertain through a secured interests search whether assets of the target company are subject to security interests;

(iv) Cambodia's system of laws remains underdeveloped. The opinions and decisions of the courts of Cambodia are not normally published or made available to the public, and the judicial interpretation of the laws of Cambodia is, therefore, uncertain. Also, enforcement of the law is inconsistent, which makes the legal analysis more challenging;

(v) Cambodia's current system and rules for land registration, titling, ownership and transfer of land are in a state of transition. Although official certificates of title which evidence ownership of immovable property are currently available, with the number of landowners in Phnom Penh and other urban centers who have obtained such titles continually increasing, some landowners may not have legal documentation of their ownership rights, making it difficult for investors to conduct a proper land title/property search.

[195] Contractual representations, warranties and indemnities are widely used to protect against potential risks identified during the due diligence process. Among such contractual provisions, only representations are specifically recognized by Cambodian law in that a party may rescind a contract for misrepresentation pursuant to Article 348 of the Civil Code. We are not aware of any court case where such contractual provisions have been tested in a Cambodian court. In light of this, the enforceability of such provisions may be challenged in court.

2.42 Role of the Courts

2.42.1 Overview

[196] At present, the judiciary consists of a number of courts of first instance located in each province and one in the Municipality of Phnom Penh, four regional Appellate Courts (in Phnom Penh, Sihanouk, Battambang and Tbong Khmum) and one Supreme Court. The Court of Appeal reviews both questions/matters of law (*Ang Chbab*) and fact (*Ang Het*), while the Supreme Court only hears questions/matters of law, with some exceptions in the case of a joint trial of the second grievance complaint, the Supreme Court may render a final decision on both law and facts. A Constitutional Council, which is not part of the judiciary, has been established to decide the constitutionality of laws and regulations.

[197] The lower courts preside over all types of legal matters, including civil, criminal, insolvency and commercial disputes. A dissatisfied litigant may appeal a municipal or provincial court's decision to the Court of Appeal, which will review both questions of law and fact. A final appeal may be taken to the Supreme Court but, generally, only on questions of law. The Supreme Court will review questions of both law and fact only in exceptional and rare circumstances. Such a rare circumstance may occur when the Supreme Court sends a case back to the Court of Appeal for further action, and the ensuing decision of the Court of Appeal is subsequently re-appealed to the Supreme Court.

[198] A significant development that has provided much greater certainty as to civil proceedings in the courts of Cambodia was the adoption of the Code of Civil Procedures on July 6, 2006. Among other things, the Code of Civil Procedures contains provisions for the recovery of certain legal costs incurred during litigation and provides greater certainty on the rules of evidence, including specific provisions relating to oral and documentary evidence, expert evidence and the discovery of evidence prior to trial.

[199] Significantly, the Code of Civil Procedures also provides for legal recognition of sales in execution, enabling successful litigants to proceed against the assets of another party in the settlement of the disputed claim.

[200] Further, rules relating to appeals are more specifically addressed. The Code of Civil Procedures provides for appeals from judgments of the Court of First Instance (*uttor* appeal), appeals from decisions of an Appellate Court (*satuk* appeal) and appeals from court rulings (*chomtoah* appeal). Court rulings are distinguished from judgments in that they are made by courts without reference to oral argument. The Code of Civil Procedures remains a relatively new body of legislation, and the courts have yet to implement and interpret all of its provisions fully. Nonetheless, it represents a significant step forward in the development of Cambodia's civil litigation procedures.

2.42.2 Mediation and Commercial Arbitration in Cambodia

[201] Historically, the courts were the only judicial, or quasi-judicial, means available in Cambodia for the resolution of commercial disputes. Certain ministries will act as a mediator on a case-by-case basis, but such mediation lacks judicial authority and, therefore, execution authority and becomes binding only if accepted mutually by the disputing parties.

[202] The government is making gradual progress in establishing other judicial and quasi-judicial forums, specifically for the resolution of commercial disputes. A law currently in draft form would create a commercial court having jurisdiction over commercial disputes.

[203] Significant recent progress has resulted in the successful launch of the NCAC. The Commercial Arbitration Law, adopted on March 6, 2006, mandated the establishment of the NCAC.

[204] The NCAC is a self-governing institution and complements the country's already-successful Arbitration Council, which hears collective labor disputes.

[205] The first group of arbitrators of the NCAC was initially selected in January 2013 and completed their initial training in 2014. The NCAC adopted its arbitration rules and internal working rules in July 2014 and its Code of Conduct of Arbitrators in April 2015. The NCAC arbitration rules are generally aligned with the arbitration rules of many well-known, reputable arbitration institutions.

[206] Under the NCAC arbitration rules, the parties to a commercial dispute are free to select their arbitrators, decide on the applicable law, determine the number of arbitrators and the language of the arbitration proceedings and decide whether the arbitration proceedings are to be conducted with or without a hearing.

[207] The awards of the NCAC are final and binding and may only be reopened for reasons of correction, amplification, interpretation or addition. The proceedings are confidential and closed to the public unless the parties agree otherwise. The arbitral tribunal may publish redacted versions of its awards unless a party objects.

[208] As a non-judicial body independent of any governmental entity, the NCAC does not have enforcement authority. As such, in order to enforce an arbitral award, the non-prevailing party must cooperate in such enforcement or, failing such cooperation, the prevailing party may seek a court order to recognize and enforce the award. *See* paragraphs [210]–[213] below for a discussion on enforcement of arbitral awards.

[209] In addition to institutional arbitration through the NCAC, the Commercial Arbitration Law formally recognizes ad hoc arbitration as a form of dispute resolution. It closely mirrors the United Nations Commission on International Trade Law (UNCITRAL) model law and makes specific provision for the enforcement of ad hoc arbitration awards by the courts.

2.42.3 Foreign Arbitration and Enforcement

[210] As mentioned above, Cambodia is a signatory to the New York Convention. Under the New York Convention, generally, arbitral awards properly issued by reputable arbitral tribunals in jurisdictions which are also parties to the New York Convention can be enforced in Cambodia. The year 2014 saw the first successful attempt at enforcement of a foreign arbitral award when the Supreme Court of Cambodia confirmed a decision of the Cambodian Court of Appeal, which ruled in favor of recognition and enforcement of an arbitral award administered by the Korean Commercial Arbitration Board (KCAB) of Seoul, South Korea.

[211] In the absence of enforcement of an arbitral award through the voluntary cooperation of the non-prevailing party, a court order recognizing and enforcing an award is necessary. Article 353 of the Code of Civil Procedures provides the mechanism by which such a court order may be sought. For arbitral awards issued domestically by the NCAC or through ad hoc arbitration, a party may file a motion with the court having territorial jurisdiction over the debtor and, if no court is determined to have such jurisdiction, then with the Court of First Instance having jurisdiction over the territory in which the property that is the object of the claim, or that can be attached, is located. The Court of Appeal has sole jurisdiction over motions seeking recognition and enforcement of foreign arbitral awards.

[212] A party seeking a court order to recognize and enforce an arbitral award must submit a motion seeking the same along with an authenticated original arbitral award or a certified copy thereof, and the original arbitration agreement or a certified copy thereof.

[213] Article 353 of the Code of Civil Procedures, which mirrors the relevant provision of the New York Convention, sets out the grounds upon which a court may deny a motion to recognize and enforce an arbitral award. Those grounds are:

- (i) a party to the arbitration was under some incapacity, or the said agreement is not valid under the governing law chosen by the parties, or in the absence of a choice of law, under the law of the country where the award was made;
- (ii) the party against whom the award is invoked was not given proper notice of the appointment of an arbitrator or of the arbitral proceedings;
- (iii) the award deals with a dispute not contemplated by or not falling within the terms of the submission to arbitration
- (iv) the composition of the arbitral tribunal or the arbitral procedure was not in accordance with the agreement of the parties or not in accordance with the law where the arbitral proceedings took place;
- (v) the award is not final;
- (vi) the subject matter of the dispute cannot be settled by arbitration; or
- (vii) recognition or enforcement of the award would be contrary to public policy.

2.42.4 Investor-State Arbitration under the ASEAN Comprehensive Investment Agreement

[214] Globally, under investment law, arbitration is often considered the primary option for foreign investors wishing to pursue claims against a host state. Provisions on investor-state dispute settlement mechanisms are incorporated within most international investment treaties and bilateral investment agreements.

[215] The ASEAN Member States have adopted the ASEAN Comprehensive Investment Agreement (ACIA) as part of the region's AEC, having a goal to transform ASEAN into a single market, a highly competitive economic region and to achieve regional economic integration. The ACIA offers a range of protections for entitled investments which are ensured by a number of obligations imposed on the Member States. These include the obligation to provide fair and equitable treatment, national and most-favored nation treatment, as well as full protection and security and the obligation to offer protection from expropriation.

[216] In order to benefit from the protections set out in the ACIA, an investment must be a "Covered Investment" as defined in Article 4(a) of the ACIA. Specifically, a "Covered Investment" is an investment made by an investor of one Member State in the territory of another Member State which has been admitted to its laws, regu lations and national policies and, where applicable, specifically approved in writing by the competent authority of the Member State.

[217] ACIA benefits apply to investors from the Member States, including both natural and juridical persons, and extends its protection to investors from outside ASEAN who set up a juridical entity in any of the Member States, provided, however, that such entity must carry out substantial business activities in the ASEAN Member State. A juridical entity which is established in a Member State, but does not carry out substantial business activities in that Member State, can be denied the protections of the ACIA in the event that such juridical entity invests in another Member State (Article 19 of the ACIA). Benefits of the ACIA can also be denied if the investor is a juridical person of a Member State but is controlled by an investor of a non-Member State. According to Article 19(3) of the ACIA, "a juridical person is 'controlled' by an investor if the investor has the power to name a majority of its directors or otherwise to legally direct its actions." These measures exist to deter the use of mere shell companies and to deter "treaty shopping" which consists of the use of a treaty contrary to its object or purpose.

[218] The ACIA requires parties to an investment dispute to try to resolve the dispute by consultation and negotiation, prior to initiating a claim whether under local courts or arbitration. If the dispute has not been resolved within 180 days of the receipt by the Member State of a request for consultations, the investor may submit their claim to the host state courts or to arbitration.

[219] Under the ACIA, an investor may submit a dispute against a Member State to the International Center for Settlement of Investment Disputes, in accordance with the arbitration rules of the UNCITRAL, to the Regional Center for Arbitration at Kuala Lumpur, or to any other arbitration institution agreed to by the parties.

3 MERGER CONTROLS, ANTITRUST/ COMPETITION ISSUES

[220] The Competition Law was promulgated on October 5, 2021, although there are significant issues that must still be determined through regulatory instruments, regulatory decisions and guidance. The Competition Law prohibits listed anti-competitive horizontal agreements and vertical minimum resale price maintenance on a per se basis and other listed anti-competitive vertical agreements and abuses of market power on a rule of reason basis (i.e., based on their anti-competitive effects or objects). The Competition Law also prohibits anti-competitive business combinations, although the details are left to Sub-Decree.

[221] The Sub-Decree on Requirements and Procedures for Business Combinations dated March 6, 2023 has been issued with immediate implementation and is to be fully effective within six months of that date. It contemplates a mandatory suspensory pre-merger notification where any of the thresholds (to be set out in a decision of the regulator) are satisfied as well as a mandatory post-merger notification in other cases. A two-stage review process is established with respect to business combinations subject to pre-merger notification.

[222] The regulator has seven working days from the date of receipt of a pre-merger notification to confirm whether it is complete and, if it is not, it will provide notice to the notifying parties identifying its concerns. From the date of receipt of a complete notification, the regulator has thirty working days to complete its preliminary review, after which, if not informed by the regulator that the proposed business combination is subject to secondary review, the transaction may be completed.

[223] If a proposed business combination is subject to secondary review, the regulator will issue a notice to that effect to the notifying parties and identify information required to conduct its secondary review. Once that information has been provided, the regulator has sixty working days to conduct its secondary review, subject to potential extensions and suspension of that period.

[224] The Sub-Decree also provides for the parties to apply to the regulator for an advance ruling certificate to be issued with respect to a proposed business combination. If issued, an advance ruling certificate: (a) serves as any required pre-merger notification; (b) permits completion of the proposed business combination and (c) prevents the regulator from challenging the business combination under Article 11 of the Competition Law for 1 year from the date of its issue.

[225] From a sectoral perspective, the Telecommunications Law dated December 17, 2015, contains provisions relating to competition issues involving telecommunications operators as well as persons involved with the telecommunications sector. There is, as yet, no guidance on how these provisions or their scope of jurisdiction will be interpreted. Further, we are not aware of any promulgating decree with respect to this law. As of writing, we are not aware of any enforcement of the competition provisions to date.

4 EMPLOYMENT CONSIDERATIONS

4.1 Legislative Framework

[226] Since its introduction on March 13, 1997, the Cambodian Labour Law, as amended on July 20, 2007 and on June 26, 2018 (Labour Law), remains the primary legislation governing all employment relationships and activities in Cambodia. The Labour Law governs the relationship between employers and employees resulting from employment contracts that are to be performed within the territory of Cambodia, regardless of where the contract was signed, the nationalities of the parties or where the parties reside and applies to every public, semi-public or private enterprise and every establishment, association or group of any nature whatsoever. In addition to the Labour Law, several types of subordinate legislation supplement the Labour Law and its enforcement.

[227] In addition, on May 17, 2016, the Law on Trade Unions entered into force and is intended to provide rights and freedom for enterprises, establishments and persons governed by the provisions of the Labour Law and persons serving in air and maritime transportation as well as to set out the organization and functioning of professional organizations of employees and employers. This law includes provisions related to, among other things, the establishment, operation, dissolution, rights and obligations and dispute resolution concerning professional organizations of employees and employers. This law also includes provisions related to employee representatives (shop stewards), employees' unions with the most representative status, termination procedures of specially protected employees and negotiation of collective bargaining agreements.

[228] Generally speaking, labor-related laws and regulations are enforced and implemented by the MLVT. Under the MLVT, there are multiple Departments of Labour and Vocational Training (DLVT) (for Phnom Penh and each province).

[229] The MLVT and the MEF jointly issued Joint Prakas 335 which outlines a clearer separation of authority between the MLVT (Central Administration) and DLVT based on factors such as the number of employees, specific sectors and locations of the enterprise. Based on Joint Prakas 335, the labor compliance documents for enterprises employing at least 101 employees or operating an export business or casino or located within a special economic zone or that are classified as 3-star resorts and hotels and above, private recruitment agencies, airlines or shipping companies, headquarters of a financial institution, headquarters of an immovable property development company or civil society organizations are under the authority of Central Administration of the MLVT. Labor compliance documents for enterprises employing up to 100 employees or which are operating resorts or hotels below three stars, branches of financial institutions, branches of immovable property development companies or branches of civil society organizations are under the authority of the DLVT. However, in practice, the determination of whether a Cambodian entity is under the MLVT or DLVT must be determined on a case-by-case basis and may require further inquiry with the MLVT and/or DLVT. Furthermore, pursuant to Prakas 430, the MLVT has launched a new online system for filing applications related to public services in relation to the labor sector. Therefore, almost all of the labor registration must now proceed via the MLVT online system.

4.2 Employment Protection

4.2.1 Overview of the Labor Registration and General Working Conditions

[230] Under the Labour Law, every enterprise is required to fulfill labor registration with the MLVT or DLVT, including:

(i) a declaration of enterprise opening;
(ii) declarations of initial employees and ongoing staff movements;

(iii) registration of an establishment book;
(iv) registration of a payroll ledger;
(v) approval of workbooks and work permits for Cambodian and foreign staff; and
(vi) approval of the foreign employee quota (capped at 10% of the total number of Cambodian staff).

Further, with respect to social security registration, as soon as an enterprise hires one employee, it is required to register itself and its employee with the National Social Security Fund (NSSF).

[231] The MLVT introduced the online system for the application of foreign employee quotas and foreign employees' work permits, which was implemented on September 1, 2016. As a result, enterprises and foreign employees can now apply for foreign employee quotas, and foreign employees' work permits through the online system.

[232] For enterprises with a large number of employees, the following additional registrations and requirements must be fulfilled:

(i) registration of internal work rules (if there are eight or more employees);
(ii) election of shop steward (if there are eight or more employees);
(iii) training of apprentices (if there are more than sixty employees);
(iv) establishment of a permanent infirmary or medical clinic and organizing nurse(s), doctor(s), medicine and other medical equipment in accordance with the relevant law and regulations (if there are fifty or more employees);
(v) employment of qualified disabled persons constituting 1% of the total workforce and reporting of the same to the MLVT and the Ministry of Social Affairs, Veteran and Youth Rehabilitation in January each year (if there are 100 or more employees);
(vi) establishment of a nursing room and a day-care center (if there are 100 or more female employees); and
(vii) establishment of a Human Immunodeficiency Virus (HIV) committee. The HIV committee's role is to promote employee awareness with respect to the prevention of the infection and spread of HIV/AIDS (acquired immune deficiency syndrome) in the workplace. We note that, in practice, few enterprises comply with this requirement and, to our knowledge, no sanctions are imposed in the case of noncompliance by an employer.

[233] General working conditions are as follows:

(i) Working hours: Normal working hours of employees are eight hours per day and forty-eight hours per week. Employers are free to establish their own working schedules for different jobs based on the type of work and how it is organized, subject to approval from the relevant authorities. It should be noted that, as of July 2021, a draft amendment of the Labour Law is being discussed and provisions relating to working shifts may be subject to amendment.

(ii) Annual leave: Full-time employees are entitled to paid annual leave accrued at the rate of one and a half working days per month of continuous service.
(iii) Special leave: Employers may grant employees special leave, not exceeding seven days per year, which shall be deducted from annual leave.
(iv) Maternity leave: Female employees are entitled to maternity leave of at least ninety days. During maternity leave, female employees are entitled to half of their regular wages, plus certain other benefits, provided that they have completed at least one year of uninterrupted service with the enterprise.
(v) Public holidays: Employees are entitled to paid public holidays in accordance with annual Prakas of the MLVT. For 2021, a total of twenty-one days of public holidays were declared by the MLVT.
(vi) Minimum age: Minimum allowable age for a salaried position is 15 years old, with the exception that persons aged from 12 to 15 years of age may be hired to do "light work." That said, no unemancipated child of either sex less than 18 years old can contract to work without the consent of their guardian.
(vii) Minimum wage: Currently, despite the fact that the Law on National Minimum Wage has been effective since July 6, 2018, there is no national minimum wage for employees except for the employees working in the garment, textile and footwear manufacturing sectors, which is USD185 for probationary employees and USD194 for regular employees for 2022. In addition, employees in these sectors are paid other mandatory benefits specific to these sectors only, such as attendance bonuses, seniority bonuses, travel and accommodation allowances and overtime meal allowances.

4.2.2 Transfer of Employees

[234] Under Article 87 of the Labour Law, if a change occurs in the legal status of an employer, particularly by succession or inheritance, sale or merger, all labor contracts in effect on the day of change remain binding between the new employer and the employees of the former enterprise. In other words, the new employer must continue to carry out the employment contracts between the affected employees and the former enterprise. The termination of an employment contract by the former employer or new employer as a consequence of any of the above circumstances constitutes a termination without a valid reason and entitles the employee to, among other things, termination compensation and damages.

[235] However, if the transaction does not trigger any change in the legal status of the employer as described above, but merely constitutes a business transfer between two distinct legal entities, there is no specific mechanism under the Labour Law for the transfer of employment contracts from one legal entity to another legal entity. As a matter of practice, the transfer can take place by terminating the existing employment contracts with the old legal entity and entering into new employment contracts with the new legal entity. In such a scenario, generally, the terminating legal entity would be required to provide termination compensation to the terminated employees in accordance with the Labour Law and the terminated employees would then commence new employment with the new legal entity without retaining their original seniority.

[236] The Labour Law allows for collective termination of employees if it is due to a reduction in an employer's activity or an internal reorganization. A collective termination is subject to certain procedures, including but not limited to: (i) the establishment of the order of termination in light of professional qualifications, seniority within the establishment and the family responsibilities of its employees; (ii) informing the staff representative in writing concerning the proposed collective termination; and (iii) informing the labor inspector of the MLVT or DLVT of each step in the collective termination process.

4.2.3 Employee Representatives and Related Obligations of the Employer

[237] The Labour Law does not require large companies to provide a seat on company boards to an employee representative.

[238] However, it is mandatory that enterprises with eight or more employees have employee representatives (or shop stewards). An employee representative is defined as the sole representative of the employees in the enterprise. Employers employing eight or more employees are required to hold elections for employee representatives and submit the election minutes to the MLVT's online system within eight days following the date of the election and post a copy of the official report of the election result within the enterprise for employees to access. The requirements of the number of employee representatives will vary depending upon the precise number of employees.

[239] An employee eligible to be a candidate for election as an employee representative or eligible to vote for the employee representative must satisfy specific criteria including having at least three months of employment seniority in the enterprise. Once elected, the employee representative(s) must be consulted concerning approval of the internal work rules of the enterprise and each subsequent amendment and with respect to redundancy measures arising from a reduction in activity or an internal reorganization of the enterprise. Elected employee representatives also enjoy special protection against termination, which means the employer needs to obtain approval from the labor inspector before being able to terminate the employee with special protection.

[240] The Labour Law does not specifically address the employer's obligation to provide information to or consult with employee representatives concerning a transfer of shares or the sale of a business. However, if a transfer of shares or the sale of a business results in a mass layoff, the employer must consult with the employee representatives concerning the redundancy measures arising from a reduction in activity or an internal reorganization of the enterprise.

[241] Employees may not be able to block the transfer of shares or the sale of a business, although it is important to note that, in the case of a mass layoff, the labor inspector must be kept informed of the process of such layoff. At the request of the

employee representatives, the labor inspector can invite the employer and employees concerned to a meeting or meetings to discuss the impact of the proposed mass layoff and measures to be taken to minimize such impact. In exceptional cases, the MLVT can issue a Prakas (ministerial order) to suspend the layoff for a period not exceeding thirty days in order to help the concerned parties find a solution. This suspension may only be exercised once by a Prakas of the MLVT.

4.2.4 Trade Union

[242] Currently, there is no "work council" in Cambodia. Besides the employee representatives, as mentioned above, the Labour Law and the Law on Trade Unions allow employees to establish or join a union. A union has three structural levels as follows:

(i) a local union: a professional organization established by at least ten employees based in the enterprise or establishment;
(ii) a union federation: a professional organization established by at least seven registered local unions with the same or similar professions or economic activities; and
(iii) a union confederation or a coalition of union federations: a professional organization established by at least five registered union federations.

[243] Without discrimination, all employees are free to form, join or withdraw themselves from a union of their own choice. To enjoy the rights and benefits under the Law on Trade Unions, a union must be registered with the MLVT. Only registered unions have legal status and legality. They have the right to sue in court, acquire movable or immovable properties and enter into contracts.

[244] Unions have a duty to engage with employers in good faith for the purpose of representing the interests of their members in determining terms and conditions of employment and in ensuring compliance with the agreed terms and conditions as well as rights in accordance with the law.

4.2.5 Employment Termination

Overview

[245] The Labour Law distinguishes between two main types of employment contracts: Fixed Duration Contracts (FDCs) and Unfixed Duration Contracts (UDCs). The termination process ultimately depends upon the type of employment contract between the employee and the employer and whether or not the termination is made with or without cause. The Labour Law, however, does not distinguish between "blue-collar workers" and "white-collar workers." Hence, the same termination procedures apply to both such workers.

[246] An FDC between an employer and an employee must be made in writing and specify the date on which employment is to commence and end. Although an FDC can be renewed, the total duration of an FDC must not exceed two years. When the entire duration of the contractual relationship exceeds two years, whether renewed or not, the FDC shall be deemed to be converted to a UDC regardless of the original intent of the contractual parties. A UDC is an employment contract that can be made verbally or in writing containing no end date and with or without a clear starting date.

Termination of an FDC

[247] An FDC will expire at its expiration date. If an FDC has a duration of more than six months, an employee must be informed of the expiration or of its non-renewal ten days in advance. The notice period is extended to fifteen days for an FDC that has a duration of more than one year. If there is no prior notice, an FDC shall be extended for a length of time equal to its initial duration or deemed to be a UDC if the total length of a contract is more than two years or the work tacitly continues after the end of an FDC.

[248] An FDC cannot be terminated before its expiration date, except:

(a) upon mutual agreement by way of a separate termination agreement, signed by both employee and employer in front of a labor inspector;
(b) when there is an event of force majeure, such as an earthquake, flood or fire; or
(c) when there is "serious misconduct" by the employee (to the extent proven by the employer).

[249] If an employer terminates an FDC on grounds (a) and (b) above, the employer is required to provide the employee with the following:

(a) severance pay of at least equal to 5% of the total salary and benefits paid to the employee during the term of the contract if there is no collective bargaining agreement that provides otherwise;
(b) compensation for unused annual leave (if any); and
(c) the last unpaid salary and other benefits (if any).

[250] Although the Labour Law is unclear and may be subject to different interpretations, in the event of serious misconduct, the employer is only required to pay compensation for any unused annual leave and the final unpaid salary and other benefits (if any).

[251] Termination of an FDC without cause occurs where termination:

(a) occurs prior to the expiration date of the contract and without the consent of the other party;
(b) is not because of serious misconduct; and
(c) is not because of an event of force majeure.

[252] If an employer terminates an FDC without cause, the Labour Law provides that the following amounts shall be payable to the employee:

(a) compensation at least equal to the remuneration the employee would have received up to the expiration date of the contract;
(b) severance pay of at least 5% of the total salary and benefits paid to the employee during the term of the contract if there is no collective bargaining agreement that provides otherwise;
(c) compensation for unused annual leave (if any); and
(d) the last unpaid salary and other benefits (if any).

Termination of a UDC

[253] A UDC is terminated with cause when it is terminated on any of the following grounds:

(a) with a valid reason relating to the employee's aptitude or behavior, based on the requirements of the operation of the enterprise;
(b) as a result of an event of force majeure; or
(c) as a result of serious misconduct by the employee.

[254] An employee whose UDC is terminated with cause (in the absence of serious misconduct) is entitled to:

(a) prior written notice of such termination (or compensation in lieu) given to the employee based on the employee's length of service as follows:

Length of Employment	*Notice Period*
< 6 months	7 (calendar) days
≥ 6 months up to and including 2 years	15 (calendar) days
> 2 years up to and including 5 years	1 (calendar) month
> 5 years up to and including 10 years	2 (calendar) months
> 10 years	3 (calendar) months

(b) two days of paid leave per week to look for a new job during the notice period;
(c) seniority payments (discussed in detail below):
    (i) *new seniority payments*: upon termination, the employer must provide new seniority pay equal to seven days of wages and other benefits to the employees if their remaining seniority for the current year (after the latest payment of new seniority pay up to the termination date) is from one month to less than six months; and

(ii) *seniority back pay (prior to 2019)*: upon termination, the employer must provide the total amount of outstanding seniority back pay equal to fifteen days of wages and benefits per year to a maximum of 156 days of wages and benefits, if any;

(d) the last unpaid salary; and
(e) compensation for unused annual leave, if any.

[255] In the event of serious misconduct, the employer is only required to pay compensation for any unused annual leave and the final unpaid salary.

[256] Under the Labour Law, upon the termination of a UDC without cause by the employer, the terminated employee is entitled to the following:

(a) two days of paid leave per week to look for a new job during the notice period;
(b) notice (or compensation in lieu) on the basis set out above;
(c) seniority pay (subject to our comments on seniority pay below);
(d) damages equal to the amount of seniority pay and, in the case of acceptance, the employee is not obliged to provide evidence of damages;
(e) the last unpaid salary and other benefits (if any); and
(f) compensation for unused annual leave, if any.

[257] Under Article 89 of the Labour Law, severance pay for a UDC is equal to seven days of salary and fringe benefits if the employees length of continuous service is from six to twelve months, or fifteen days of salary and fringe benefits (to a maximum of six months of salary and fringe benefits) per year of service if the employee has worked for an employer for more than one year. The Amendment to the Labour Law replaces certain articles (including Article 89) of the Labour Law. Under Article 89 of the Labour Law, "severance pay" (or indemnity for dismissal) was payable only upon termination of a UDC by an employer, except for serious misconduct committed by an employee. However, from 2019 onwards, "severance pay" will be replaced with "seniority payments," which must be paid to UDC employees every six months. When the Amendment to the Labour Law came into effect on June 26, 2018, the MLVT issued Prakas 443 dated September 21, 2018, outlining the scope and procedures to effect the seniority payments for employees under the UDCs (including the new seniority payments from 2019 onwards and retroactive payments for past seniority prior to 2019), which came into effect from January 1, 2019 except the retroactive payments (Back Pay) for enterprises outside of the garment, textile and footwear manufacturing sectors that have been delayed to December 2021 by the MLVT in its Guideline 042/19 dated March 22, 2019, upon which the employer is required to Back Pay equal to three days of based wages in June and three days of based on wages in December until the outstanding Back Pay is paid off. In light of the above, starting from January 1, 2019, if an employer terminates an employee under a UDC, the employer will have to follow the procedures for "seniority payments" under the new law, as opposed to procedures for "severance pay" under the old law.

Seniority pay after 2018 (New Seniority Pay) equal to fifteen days of wages and fringe benefits per year must be paid to employees during ongoing employment every six months per year, divided into 7.5 days of wages and other benefits to be paid in June and 7.5 days of wages and other benefits to be paid in December. For the first year of employment, an employee who works from one to six consecutive months (up to the end of each semester, either June or December) is entitled to New Seniority Pay of 7.5 days of wages and benefits. In addition to the New Seniority Pay, employees who were employed prior to 2019 are also entitled to the Back Pay for all their past seniority. The amount of the Back Pay is, however, capped at a maximum of 156 days of the average base wages in each of the relevant years of employment up to December 31, 2018. Employees in all other sectors besides textile, garment, and footwear who have worked prior to January 1, 2019 and remain working for an enterprise, will be entitled to 15 days of Back Pay per year (to a maximum of six months or 156 days) paid 7.5 days of Back Pay to be paid in June each year and 7.5 days of Back Pay to be paid in December each year.

[258] In addition, if an employee commits an act that constitutes serious misconduct, the employer will be considered to have waived its right to dismiss such employee if such right is not exercised within seven days from the date on which the employer first learns of the serious misconduct in question. For other misconduct, an employer must initiate disciplinary actions within fifteen days after it ascertains that an employee has committed misconduct which forms the basis for dismissal. If an employer does not initiate such actions within the fifteen-day period, it may not take any disciplinary actions against the employee for that misconduct.

Employees with Special Protection

[259] The following employees are entitled to special protection within a certain period of time:

(a) employee representatives—protected during their terms of position (two years for each term) and three months after the end of their terms;
(b) unelected candidates for employee representative elections—protected for three months after the result of shop stewards election;
(c) three elected union leaders of legally registered unions—protected during their terms of position (the Law on Trade Union does not mention about the duration of the terms. In practice, it can be up to four years);
(d) founding union members or normal union members—protected from the date of submission of applications of union registration until thirty days after the union is duly registered; and
(e) candidates (both elected and unelected) for union elections—protected within forty-five days before and after the union election.

[260] The termination of employees entitled to special protection requires prior approval from the labor inspector. In case of serious misconduct, prior approval from the MLVT is required before termination may be effected. If the labor inspector disagrees with the ground for termination, the suspension shall be deemed invalid, and the employee shall be reinstated and back-paid for the period of suspension.

4.2.6 NSSF

[261] The NSSF scheme covers three pillars: (i) health insurance; (ii) retirement pension; and (iii) occupational risk insurance. The NSSF has implemented the occupational risk insurance scheme since 2008, followed by the introduction 2016 of health insurance. The pension component of the scheme will be implemented in 2022. Employers are obliged to start remitting pension contributions to the NSSF from October 2022.

The scheme is managed by the NSSF, a public establishment to which all employers, employees and workers must pay contributions. The work-related accident insurance scheme and health care insurance scheme are currently fully operational.

[262] The occupational risk insurance scheme covers employees and workers in case of a work-related accident or illness caused by the occupation (both are considered "labor risks"). The employer is required to provide the employee or worker with certain benefits, care and treatment, depending on the circumstances. An accident is considered to be work-related, regardless of the cause, if it happens to an employee or worker in the workplace or during the direct commute to and from the workplace. If the victim requires hospital treatment, he or she must be sent to one of the listed, approved hospitals. The related Prakas has set out the procedure for registering enterprises and their employees with the NSSF and have determined the rate of contribution to be paid with respect to the work-related injury component of the scheme.

[263] In October 2008, the NSSF issued a notification clarifying the timeframe for payment of NSSF contributions. It also sets out a number of important details regarding which hospitals the victims of work-related injuries may be sent to and details regarding the claim procedure.

[264] Employers or enterprise owners employing one or more employees are obliged to register their business and its local and foreign employees with the NSSF. An enterprise which was in operation but had not yet registered with the NSSF was required to register with the NSSF by December 10, 2017. A newly established enterprise must register its employee(s) with the NSSF within thirty days after the commencement of its commercial operations. Further, an enterprise must register its employee(s) within three days after the commencement of employment, except where the employee(s) already holds an NSSF membership card. Each registered enterprise must report to the NSSF the number of employees by the 20th of every month. Each enterprise is required to pay its first monthly contribution to the NSSF within thirty days after the issuance date of the NSSF registration certificate and to pay the next contribution by the fifteenth day of the following month. The contribution to the occupational risk insurance scheme ranges from USD0 4–USD2 4 per employee per month, which is paid by the employer to the NSSF.

[265] On January 6, 2016, a health care scheme was introduced by Sub-Decree 01/16. The benefits of the health care scheme include preventive health service, treatment and medical care service and daily allowances during work suspension resulting from disease treatment or accidents other than occupational risk and maternity leave. These benefits are applicable to persons covered by the provisions of the Labour Law, including spouses and dependent children of workers who are members of the NSSF and NSSF members who are receiving a pension resulting from the permanent disability and survivors. Starting from January 1, 2018, an employer must register its informal workers for the health care scheme with the NSSF and female workers, whether informal or formal, are entitled to additional allowance after delivery of their child from the NSSF, funded by the State's budget. The contribution to the health care insurance scheme is the sole responsibility of the employer, and it ranges from USD1 3–USD7 8 per employee per month.

[266] On March 4, 2021, Sub-Decree 32 on the Social Security Scheme on the Pension Fund for Persons under the Scope of the Labour Law dated March 4, 2021 ("*Sub-Decree 32*") was issued aiming to implement the pension scheme and determine (among others) the mechanisms, conditions and procedures for registration, contributions and benefits under the pension scheme. Among others, it sets out that the contributions to the compulsory pension scheme are made jointly by both employers and employees with 2% each from the employee and employer for the first phase (the first five years). To supplement Sub-Decree 32, the RGC issued Sub-Decree 144 on the Determination of Contributable Wage dated August 19, 2021, which sets out the contributable wage for the pension scheme ranging from KHR400 000 (approximately USD100)–KHR1 200 000 (approximately USD300). This range may be changed at the initiative of the Board of Council of the NSSF. As such, the monthly contribution is equivalent to 4% of the employee's contributable wage (with 2% to be paid by the employee and 2% to be paid by the employer) with a range of USD4–USD12 per month per employee for the first five years.

Though the NSSF pension scheme has yet to be implemented, some large enterprises do provide certain retirement benefits to their employees through their own voluntary internal pension plans.

[267] Further, some employees have taken out pension plans from third-party providers such as insurance companies though, to our knowledge, this practice is still quite uncommon.

[268] Given that the NSSF pension scheme has not yet been implemented and, to our knowledge, there are very few companies that provide internal pension plans to their employees, problems with regard to pension schemes or other pension commitments or promises seldom arise in the context of M&A transactions in Cambodia.

[269] However, based on our experience, for the few large enterprises that do have in place such plans (which are separate and independent from the statutory NSSF pension scheme), potential issues may arise with respect to the deduction of employees' salaries for payment towards such plans (considering that such deduction is not mandated by law) and how the pension benefits are to be provided if an employment contract is terminated before the determined retirement age or when the NSSF pension scheme comes into force in the future.

[270] Further, if the seller has put in place an internal pension plan for its employees, it raises the question of how the accrued benefits attributable to an employee's former employment with the seller can be transferred to the buyer if the employee is subsequently transferred to the buyer entity pursuant to an M&A transaction.

4.3 Retention of Key Management and Employees

[271] With respect to the retention of key management and employees by the purchaser in an M&A transaction, please refer to paragraphs [234]–[236] above (Transfer of Employees).

[272] Article 70 of the Labour Law broadly prohibits an employer from imposing any restrictions on the employee after his or her employment has ceased by providing as follows:

> Any clause of a contract that prohibits a worker from engaging in any activity after the expiration of the contract is null and void.

[273] Notwithstanding, given the lack of publicly available judicial opinions and guidance on the application of Article 70 of the Labour Law, we note that, in practice, non-solicitation and non-compete covenants are commonly used in employment contracts in Cambodia.

4.4 Treatment of Foreign Employees

4.4.1 Restrictions on Foreign Employees

[274] There are no nationality, residency or professional requirements with respect to the appointment of a manager or director, local or foreign. Pursuant to Article 120 of the LCE, any legally competent natural person over 18 years of age may serve as a director or officer of a company. Each director of a limited liability company must not be a current civil servant of the Cambodian government or have been disqualified from acting as a director of a limited liability company in Cambodia (or otherwise have a criminal history). Unless the AOIs require otherwise, a director is not required to meet any other specific qualifications.

[275] Further, generally, foreign employees are not restricted from working in Cambodia except for employment in certain professions (such as tour guides, lawyers and statutory auditors), which are reserved for Cambodian nationals only.

[276] However, investors are only allowed to employ foreign employees whose qualifications, skills and expertise are not available among Cambodian citizens (the quota for which is generally capped at 10% of the employer's total local workforce).

[277] To be lawfully employed in Cambodia, a foreign employee is required to fulfill the following conditions:

(i) holds a work permit issued by the MLVT;
(ii) has entered Cambodia legally;
(iii) holds a valid passport;
(iv) has a valid residency permit;
(v) has the physical qualifications for the job; and
(vi) has no contagious diseases.

4.4.2 Ordinary Visa or E Type Visa (Visa E)

[278] Foreign nationals intending to undertake ordinary work in Cambodia must obtain a Visa E in advance from the embassies and consulates of Cambodia located in foreign countries, or (subject to restrictions on certain nationalities) "on arrival" when entering Cambodia. This visa has an initial validity of thirty days but can be extended as follows following arrival in Cambodia:

Initial Visa	*Sub-categories*	*Validity of Stay upon Extension*
(Visa E with a validity of 3 months starting from the date of issuance for stay of up to 1 month)	**E** B (for employees/ laborers/merchants)	1, 3, 6 or 12 months
	E G (for general non-immigrant foreigners)	1, 3 or 6 months (can be extended once only)
	E p (for non-immigrant foreigners wishing to explore business opportunities in Cambodia)	1 or 3 months (can be extended once only)
	E R (for non-immigrant foreign retirees)	1, 3, 6 or 12 months
	E s (for foreign students)	1, 3, 6 or 12 months
	E T (for technical personnel)	24 months, plus up to 3 further extensions of 12 months each

4.4.3 Foreign Employee Quota

[279] Enterprises employing or intending to employ foreign employees are required to apply for quota approval through the MLVT's centralized online system. Under the quota system, a maximum of 10% of an employer's total workforce may be foreign, comprised of: (i) office employees (3%); (ii) skilled labor employees (6%); and (iii) unskilled labor (1%). This quota may be increased, at the discretion of the MLVT, if an enterprise requires employees with specific skills that are currently unavailable in Cambodia. All subsequent quota applications must also be submitted before the end of November each year. Upon receipt of the approval, the employer generally cannot request the quota to be changed during the course of a year.

[280] The official timeframe to obtain a foreign employee quota approval is twenty days from the date of submission of all required documents.

[281] The official fee for the application of a foreign employee quota is KHR85 000 (approximately USD21 25), and each enterprise must also pay to E-Solution (Cambodia) Co., Ltd. (E-Solution), a third-party service provider responsible for operating the MLVT's centralized online system, a service fee of KHR115 000 (approximately USD28 75) per quota application.

4.4.4 Employment Card and Work Permit

[282] After obtaining the foreign employee quota approval, the enterprise is required to apply for an employment card and work permit (collectively, "Work Permit") for each foreign employee. The Work Permit of a foreign employee can also be applied for through the MLVT's centralized online system. The Work Permit is valid for one year. Regardless of the timing of issuance of the Work Permit, it expires on December 31 each year. If the enterprise continues to employ the same foreigners in Cambodia for the following year, the enterprise needs to apply for an extension of their Work Permits by March 31 of the following year.

[283] The official timeframe to obtain a Work Permit is twenty working days from the date of submission of all required documents.

[284] The official fee for the application or renewal of a Work Permit is KHR405 000 (approximately USD101 25). In addition, a service fee of KHR115 000 (approximately USD28 75) USD28 75 is required to be paid to E-Solution.

[285] A regulation jointly issued by the MLVT and the MEF in June 2016 clearly demonstrates MLVT's serious commitment to strengthening compliance inspection and to imposing monetary fines on enterprises that violate the Labour Law, including hiring foreign employees that do not possess valid Work Permits.

4.4.5 Health Certificate

[286] As a prerequisite to an employment card and work permit application, a foreign employee is required to undertake a health check and obtain a health certificate from the Labour Medical Department of the MLVT or at any healthcare facility at the capital or provincial level that is duly recognized by the Ministry of Health and collaborating partners of the Labour Medical Department of the MLVT. However, according to Prakas No. 352 issued by the MLVT regarding the use of an automated data management system for foreign workers, when applying for a new or for an extension of a foreign employee work permit, the foreign employee may use his/her own valid health certificate but such certificate must first be certified by the Labour Medical Department of the MLVT by paying a fee of KHR20 000 (approximately USD5) via the MLVT's centralized online system.

[287] A foreign employee is required to undergo a health check every year, regardless of whether he/she changes the workplace in order to apply for a work permit. A local employee may undergo a health check at any healthcare facility in a capital city or province, but employers must request certification of such health certificate from the Labour Medical Department through the MLVT's online system by attaching the employee's health check results (which must be treated as confidential) with a validity period of up to six months. Under Prakas 429 dated December 31, 2021, the MLVT also requires that local employees must undergo a health check once every two years except for those in certain categories or professions that require other special health checks (such as those engaging in high occupational risks). The local employees are also required to undergo a new health check if they change their work to a new one with different working conditions.

4.4.6 Social Security Contributions

[288] Please refer to paragraphs [261]–[270] above (the NSSF) which equally applies to foreign employees.

5 TAXATION ASPECTS

5.1 Overview

[289] Prior to January 1, 2016, Cambodia had three types of tax regimes, namely: (i) the real regime; (ii) the simplified regime; and (iii) the estimated regime. Taxpayers who were not sole proprietorships were subject to the real regime system. A sole proprietorship was regarded as a real regime taxpayer if its level of turnover or type of business activity met the conditions stated in the tax regulations.

[290] In December 2015, the Law on Financial Management was promulgated and with it, the abolition of the simplified and estimated regimes of taxation in Cambodia.

[291] Since January 1, 2016, there has been only one regime of taxation in Cambodia, i.e., the real regime. The real regime has been renamed as the self-assessment regime and amended to create three categories of the taxpayer:

Self-Assessed Regime	*Criteria*
SMALL TAXPAYER	A small taxpayer is any sole proprietorship or partnership that: – Has annual turnover* from KHR250 million (USD62 500)–KHR1 000 million (USD250 000) for agricultural, service and commercial sectors; – Has annual turnover from KHR250 million (USD62 500)–KHR1 600 million (USD400 000) for the industrial sector; – Has had, or expects to have, turnover in any period of three consecutive calendar months**, exceeding KHR60 million (USD15 000) – Participates in any bidding or quotation for the supply of goods and services.
MEDIUM TAXPAYER	A medium taxpayer includes any sole proprietorship or partnership that has: – Annual turnover from KHR1 000 million (USD250 000)–KHR4 billion (USD1 000 000) for taxpayers in the agricultural sector; – Annual turnover form KHR1 000 million (USD 250 000)–KHR6 000 million (USD1 500 000) for taxpayers in the service and commercial sectors; – Annual turnover from KHR1 600 million (USD400 000)–KHR8 000 (USD2 000 000) in the industrial sector; A medium taxpayer also includes: – Enterprises incorporated as legal entities or as a representative office; – National and sub-national government institutions, associations or non-governmental organizations, or projects under these institutions; – Foreign embassies and consulates, international organizations and technical cooperation agencies of other countries.

Self-Assessed Regime	*Criteria*
LARGE TAXPAYER	A large taxpayer includes a sole proprietorship, partnership or legal entity that has: – Annual turnover above KHR4 000 million (USD250 000) for taxpayers in the agricultural sector; (Companies/Sole Prop/Partnership) – Annual turnover 6,000 million (USD1 500 000) for taxpayers in the service and commercial sectors; – Annual turnover above KHR8 000 (USD2 000 000) in the industrial sector; A large taxpayer also includes: – Branches of foreign companies; – Subsidiary of multinational companies, – Enterprises registered as Qualified Investment Projects (*QIP*)***

*The term "turnover" refers to the level of a taxable supply of goods and services related to a taxpayers business activities.

**Calendar months: Within the same tax year.

***As approved by the Council for the Development of Cambodia.

Under Prakas 007 the GDT now has the authority to re-determine the classification of a taxpayer if the declared turnover does not reflect actual turnover. In this circumstance, a taxpayer will be classified using the value of their assets (current and non-current) as follows:

SMALL TAXPAYER	A sole proprietorship or partnership that: – Has assets valued at KHR200 million (USD50 000)–KHR1 000 million (USD250 000) in the agricultural, service and commercial sectors; – Has assets valued at KHR200 million (USD50 000)–KHR2 000 million (USD500 000) for the industrial sector.

MEDIUM TAXPAYER	A sole proprietorship, partnership or legal entity that: – Has assets valued at KHR1 000 million (USD250 000)–KHR2 000 million (USD500 000) for taxpayers in the agricultural, services and commercial sectors; – Assets valued at KHR2 000 million (USD500 000)–KHR4 000 million (USD1 000 000) in the industrial sector;
LARGE TAXPAYER	– Assets valued above KHR2 000 million (USD500 000) for taxpayers in the agricultural, services and commercial sectors; – Assets valued above KHR4 000 million (USD1 000 000) industrial

[292] Taxpayers under the self-assessment system are liable to the following taxes:[2]

- (i) Annual Taxes:
  - (a) TOI; and
  - (b) Minimum Tax (MT).
- (ii) Monthly Taxes:
  - (a) Prepayment of Income Tax (PIT);
  - (b) WHT;
  - (c) Tax on Salary (TOS); and
  - (d) Value-Added Tax (VAT).
- (iii) Other Significant Taxes:
  - (a) PT;
  - (b) Specific Tax on Certain Merchandise and Services (ST);
  - (c) Accommodation Tax (AT);
  - (d) Tax on Public Lighting (TPL);
  - (e) Tax on Unused Land;
  - (f) Tax on Immovable Property; and
  - (g) Additional Tax on Dividend Distribution (ATDD).

[2] Small real regime taxpayers are able to follow a simplified accounting system as outlined in Prakas No. 1820 MEF.Prk dated Dec. 25, 2015 on Method and Procedure on Implementation of Simple Accounting Record for Small Real Regime Taxpayers. The simplified accounting system provides prescribed rules on recording expenses, depreciable assets, WHT requirements and income recognition that may differ from the general rules as outlined in this Chapter that apply to medium and large real regime taxpayers. References to Self-Assessment Taxpayers (SAT) in this chapter refer to medium and large taxpayers.

5.2 Annual Taxes

[293] At the end of each taxable year, Self-Assessment Taxpayers (SAT) taxpayers pay either the TOI or the MT, whichever is greater.

5.2.1 TOI

[294] TOI with a standard rate of 20%. Special tax rates apply to taxpayers in extraction or insurance industries. TOI is imposed on a resident taxpayer's worldwide income.

5.2.2 Rates of TOI

[295]

Business Types	*Tax Rates*
Legal entities (general businesses)	20%
Qualified Investment Project (tax exemption period)	0%
Oil or natural gas production sharing contract, or realized in the exploitation of natural resources.	30%
Insurance companies	5% on insurance or re-insurance premium on life with saving characteristics and other activities

The TOI (previously referred to as Tax on Profit) is the regular Cambodian corporate income tax. It is imposed at the standard rate of 20% and applies to legal entities that are incorporated under the laws of Cambodia.

Taxable income is the net income from all types of business operations including capital gains realized, interest, rental income, royalty income and income from financial or investment activities, including investments in immovable assets. Foreign exchange gains, when realized, are also taxable.

Taxable income is calculated by adjusting the accounting income in accordance with the requirements of the LOT.

As a general rule, expenses are deductible if they are paid or incurred in a tax year to carry on the business of the taxpayer. Any expense reasonably connected with the running of the business may be deducted. Realized foreign exchange losses are also deductible. Note that Article 33 of Prakas 098 provides that "expenses linked to abnormal management," expenses that "provide benefits to third parties," "expenses for personal needs" and "extravagant expenses" are not deductible for tax purposes in Cambodia.

Tax Loss Carry Forward

[296] Losses can be carried forward for a maximum of five years. Losses cannot be carried back. Losses must be deducted from the first following year in which an enterprise makes a profit. If the profit is not sufficient to deduct the entire loss, the remainder of the loss after deduction can be carried forward to deduct from the profit in following years for up to five years. If the company incurs a loss in more than one year, the enterprise must deduct each loss in sequential order.

In order for the carry-forward loss to be deductible:

(a) the tax loss must be recorded in the tax return which has been submitted to the tax administration;
(b) the taxpayer must not have received a unilateral tax assessment from the tax authorities; and
(c) there is no change in the business objectives of the company.

Tax Depreciation

[297] Under Cambodian law, expenses must be borne by the Company in order to be deductible for TOI purposes. Furthermore, expenses can be classified as being either operational expenditure to be deducted against the income derived in the period in which they were actually incurred, or as capital expenditure to be recorded in the relevant asset account in the balance sheet and depreciated over its useful life.

Under Cambodian tax law, before an asset can be depreciated, it must meet all five conditions:

(a) depreciation must be made only on a fixed asset recorded in the balance sheet of the enterprise;
(b) depreciation must be made only on a fixed asset subject to depreciation;
(c) depreciation must be made on the basis and within the scope of cost price;
(d) depreciation must be calculated in accordance with the straight-line method of depreciation for Class 1 assets or the declining balance method of depreciation for Classes 2, 3 and 4 assets (detail below); and
(e) depreciation must be made actually by an enterprise.

Depreciation deductions are provided with respect to tangible and intangible property used in the operation of a business. The depreciation rates for tangible property are as follows:

(a) *Class 1*: Constructions including Building (the concrete building), structure of the structures, including their basic components, roads, railways, transport ship—*5%* depreciation rate based on *straight-line* method.
(b) *Class 1*: Building (the non-concrete building)—*10%* depreciation rate based on *straight-line* method.
(c) *Class 2*: Computers, electronic information systems, software and data handling equipment—*50%* depreciation rate based on *declining balance method.*

(d) *Class 3*: Automobiles, trucks and office furniture & equipment—*25%* depreciation rate based on *declining balance method*. and
(e) *Class 4*: All other tangible property—*20%* depreciation rate based on *declining balance method*.

Assets in Classes 2–4 are accounted for on a pooled basis, and therefore profits and losses on disposals are not directly recognized for tax purposes. Additions are depreciated for a full year in the year of acquisition. Please note that land is not a depreciable asset.

Intangible property such as patents, copyrights, drawings, models or franchises are subject to straight-line depreciation. Intangible assets with known limited asset life will be depreciated based on the life of the asset. If the life of the intangible cannot be determined, the depreciation rate will be 10%.

Deductibility of Interest

[298] There is no thin capitalization rule nor any debt-to-equity requirements under the Cambodia tax rules. However, Article 12 of the LOT and Article 32 of Prakas 098 impose a limit on interest deduction, stating that interest expense is deductible up to the sum of interest income and 50% of the net non-interest income and 100% of its interest income for the applicable tax year.

The term "*net non-interest income*" is the gross income other than interest income, reduced by the allowable expenses except for interest expense. In other words, a taxpayer is permitted to deduct payments of interest expenses up to a cap which is the sum of 50% of the taxpayer's net profit (exclusive of interest expenses and interest income) plus 100% of the interest income received or receivable in the taxable year. The interest expense disallowed as a deduction in the current tax years may be carried forward as an interest expense to succeeding years for deductions under the same limitation until the fifth year from when the interest occurred.

Based on instruction 11946 dated August 21, 2018, loan agreements between related parties do not need to be registered with the GDT as per Circular 151.

Further, the GDT issued Circular 4909 dated March 18, 2019 stating the required documents to support the interest charge of the related party loan. Enterprises are required to maintain and provide the following documents to the tax administration to support the interest charged under a related party loan even if the interest charged is different from the market interest rate:

(a) loan agreement stating the specific borrowing period;
(b) business plan related to the borrowing;
(c) documents explaining the basis of the interest determination; and
(d) board resolution passed in relation to the borrowing.

1. Minimum Tax ("MT")

[299] MT is imposed at the rate of 1% on annual turnover inclusive of all taxes except VAT. The MT is paid for any tax year and must be reduced by the income tax actually paid in the tax year.

MT will apply in cases where:

(1) the enterprise is in a loss position; or
(2) the enterprise's 1% MT is higher than 20% of the company's TOI liability; or
(3) the enterprise does not keep a proper record of accounts.

If the TOI liability calculated is greater than the MT, the enterprise needs only to pay TOI, and any Prepayment Tax on Income liability during the year can be offset against the TOI liability.

For Item 3 above, the GDT clarified in Prakas 638 dated July 4, 2017 what constitutes an improper accounting records:

(a) enterprises with accounting records which do not meet the requirements set out by the GDT and the Ministry of Economy and Finance ("*MEF*");
(b) enterprises which fail to issue invoices for business transactions as stated in Articles 77, 79 and 98 of the LOT;[3]
(c) enterprises which commit serious negligence as stated in Article 126[4] of the LOT;
(d) enterprises which commit tax evasion as stated in Article 127[5] of the LOT; and
(e) enterprises which do not have an audit report from independent auditors if their annual turnover is more than KHR2 billion (approximately USD500 000).

QIPs are not automatically exempted from the MT. Under the New Investment Law they need to evidence that they have an audit report from independent auditors.

2. Prepayment of Tax on Income ("PTOI")

[300] This tax applies to taxpayers under the self-assessment regime and is required to be paid on a monthly basis at the rate of 1% of monthly turnover (inclusive of all taxes, except VAT) realized in the previous month.

---

3 Article 77 of the LOT referred to criteria for Value Added Tax Invoice. Articles 79 and 98 of the LOT referred to the taxpayer's obligation to keep books of account, supporting documents, and other financial documents for a period of ten years starting from the end of tax year.

4 Article 126 of the LOT states regarding serious negligence that "The taxpayer or withholding agent is considered seriously negligent if the amount of tax paid is less than the amount of tax as determined by tax provisions by more than 10 percent."

5 Article 127 of the LOT states about tax evasion that "Tax evasion is the willful, knowing, or systematic and repeated violation of tax provisions with the intention of reducing or eliminating the tax amount required by tax provisions to be paid.

Shall be considered also as tax evasion any serious negligence as stated in article 126 of this law which is committed on:

i. two separate occasions within a period of three calendar years;
ii. three or more separate occasions in any period of time."

Based on Prakas 098, the term "turnover" includes the income from the business activity of the taxpayer and the subsidiary income. The term "subsidiary income" includes:

(a) Income from the lease of immovable property even if the immovable property is not related to the business activity of the company.
(b) Free use of immovable property by third party is deemed as a taxable income based on the market rental fee.
(c) Free use of immovable property by the employee of the company for a private purpose except for the free common use of immovable property provided to the employee in accordance with Labor Law Provisions.
(d) Royalty—Income from the business on other intangible properties such as patent, copyright, model, design, franchise, trademark, formula etc.
(e) Other subsidiary incomes including the sale of scrap, rent of business equipment and packing.

Any payments made throughout the year can be used to offset the annual TOI or MT liabilities due at the annual tax declaration.

Note that a taxpayer will still be required to pay the monthly 1% PTOI even though they qualify for the MT exemption under Prakas 638 (as stated in Item (b) above). Any unused PTOI can be carried forward to the next year as a tax credit until the business is profitable. Nevertheless, QIP entities are exempted from the payment of PTOI for income generated from QIP activities during their TOI exemption period.

3. Withholding Tax ("WHT")

[301] WHT regulations require resident taxpayers to withhold tax on payments in cash or in kind made to resident and non-resident taxpayers. The tax must be remitted to the GDT on a monthly basis by the 20th day of the month for manual filing or the 25th day of the following month for E-filing. The following payments are subject to WHT:

Payment by a resident taxpayer to residents on:

(a) performance of services—15% (except payment to a tax-registered taxpayer and supported by a valid VAT invoice);
(b) interest—15% (except domestic bank and saving institution);
(c) royalties—15%;
(d) rental—10%;
(e) interest paid by a domestic bank or saving institution to a resident taxpayer holding a fixed term account—6%; and
(f) interest paid by a domestic bank or saving institution to a resident taxpayer holding a non-fixed term account—4%.

Payment by a resident taxpayer to non-residents

[302] Under Prakas 098, the following payments are considered to be Cambodian-sourced income and will be subject to 14% WHT when paid by a resident taxpayer to a non-resident:

(a) interest;
(b) dividends;
(c) income from services performed in Cambodia;
(d) compensation for management and technical fees;
(e) rental and other incomes connected to use of movable and immovable property;
(f) royalties;
(g) gain from the sale of immovable property located in Cambodia or profit from the transfer of benefits of immovable properties located in Cambodia or capital gains from financial and investment assets in Cambodia or capital gains from the transfer of shares in whole or in part in the capital of an enterprise;
(h) premiums for the Insurance or reinsurance of risks (The WHT does not apply on payment of premiums for the reinsurance of property and other risks in Cambodia);
(i) gains from the sale of movable property which is part of the business property of a permanent establishment maintained by a non-resident; and
(j) income from business activities carried on by a non-resident through a permanent establishment in Cambodia.

Please note that WHT does not apply to the following payments:

(a) payment of goods;
(b) payment for the supply of any service to individual or non-registered taxpayers in Cambodia under KHR50 000;
(c) payment in cash or in kind among taxpayers through a self-assessment regime must be exempted from the withholding tax in the following cases provided that there are valid VAT invoices including:
    (i) income from service providers such as management or consulting or comparable services;
    (ii) revenue from the following supplies:
        (1) shrink-wrap software;
        (2) site license;
        (3) downloadable software; and
        (4) software bundled with computer hardware;
    (iii) income from movable or immovable property rental;
(d) payment covered by an exemption under a relevant double tax agreement with Cambodia.

The WHT applies to any expense that is recorded in the Company's account whether paid or accrued. In addition, the WHT must be calculated/withheld before the payment is made to either resident or non-resident taxpayers.

Please note that, if the payer/WHT agent fails to withhold the tax before a payment is made, then the WHT is a non-deductible expense of the payer. In addition, "gross up" method is not allowed to calculate the WHT. However, such WHT can be deductible provided that the grossed-up amount (including the WHT component) is reflected in the invoice or agreement.

A WHT relief or exemption may apply under the relevant DTAs with Cambodia. However, a prior approval from the GDT is required before availing the benefits under the DTA.

Cambodian taxes covered under the DTAs include corporate income tax, withholding taxes, and tax on salary. The DTA may reduce the WHT for payments of interest, dividend, management and technical service fees and dividends to non-residents. In most cases, the DTAs will reduce the WHT rate from 14% to 10%. However, the application of DTA benefits is not automatic and must be applied for a confirmatory ruling with the GDT.

Currently, Cambodia has signed DTAs with eleven countries: Singapore, China, Brunei, Thailand, Vietnam, Indonesia, Hong Kong, Malaysia, the Republic of South Korea, Macau Special Administrative Region of the People's Republic of China and Turkey. Nine of them are now in effect (with the exception of Macau and Turkey)

4. Value Added Tax ("VAT")

[303] Under the VAT regulations, the standard VAT rate is 10% for the supplies of goods and services. Zero percent VAT rate (0% VAT) is applied for:

(i) export goods and service goods exported from Cambodia, and services performed and consumed outside Cambodia (exports are defined to include the international transportation of passengers or goods, or services in connection therewith); and
(ii) supporting industries or sub-contractors who supply certain goods and services to exporters (e.g., the garment manufacturing, textile and footwear industries), subject to certain criteria.

VAT applies to taxable supply of goods and services. The VAT rate is generally at 10% of the value of the supply of goods and services.

There is an output-input VAT mechanism under the VAT regulations. VAT-registered taxpayers can offset the output VAT they have charged to their customers with the input VAT they have paid to their suppliers. However, no input VAT can be claimed on the following expenditures:

(i) entertainment expenses;
(ii) products or imports of certain petroleum products;
(iii) purchases or imports of passenger motor vehicles; and
(iv) mobile telephone calls.

VAT-registered taxpayers are required to remit the surplus VAT to the GDT after deducting the input VAT paid to their suppliers. If the taxpayer's input VAT for the month exceeds its output VAT (i.e., VAT credit), the taxpayer is allowed to carry forward the excess VAT paid into the succeeding period. Please note that this carry-forward mechanism for VAT is applicable to taxpayers classified as Medium or Large Taxpayers only.

Under the Cambodian self-assessment tax regime, there are three classes of taxpayers which consist of small taxpayers, medium taxpayers, and large taxpayers.

VAT on E-Commerce

[304] Sub Decree No. 65 implements certain provisions covering the supply of goods and services traded through "Electronic Commerce" (e-commerce) in Cambodia. This Sub Decree is effective from April 8, 2021 and the detailed rules and procedures to implement this Sub Decree have been determined under Prakas 542 dated January 8, 2021 which was issued by the MEF.

The term "*Digital goods*" refers to intangible goods purchased, supplied, and sent entirely online, while "*Digital service*" refers to services performed online. The term "E-commerce" refers to the purchase, sale, and rental, exchange of goods or services, including commercial activity online.

The Sub Decree provides a detailed list of e-commerce transactions which include, but are not limited to, the supply of software and other services related thereto, online shopping portal or auctions, advertising, website hosting, data retrieval, consumption of digital products and/or contents via download, real-time streaming, subscription, or other means.

Non-resident taxpayers who supply digital goods or services in Cambodia with no PE who have an annual turnover KHR250 million (USD62 500) or more or expect to have a turnover of KHR60 million (USD15 000) in any three (3) consecutive months in a calendar year are required to register with the GDT following the simplified VAT registration before April 1, 2022.

For Business to Consumer *(B2C)* e-commerce transactions, the non-resident taxpayer must declare and pay the VAT on the transaction to the GDT by no later than the 20th day (for manual filing) or the 25th day (for E-filing) of the following month.

For Business to Business *(B2B)* e-commerce transactions, the VAT must be paid through a "reverse charge" mechanism. Under the "reverse charge" mechanism, the resident taxpayer receiving the supply from the non-resident taxpayer must account for and pay for the output VAT on such supply on behalf of the non-resident taxpayer. The resident taxpayer can claim the VAT paid as input tax credits in its VAT reporting.

5. Tax on Salary ("TOS")

[305] Resident taxpayers are subject to tax on their worldwide salary income (i.e., Cambodian and foreign employment income) while non-resident taxpayers are taxed on Cambodia source income only. Resident taxpayers earning foreign salary income can receive credits from foreign taxes paid.

Individuals are classified either as resident or non-resident taxpayers depending on their residence, place of abode or presence in Cambodia. An individual is deemed to be a resident if they are resident or have a principal place of abode in Cambodia, or are present in Cambodia for more than 182 days in any 12-month period ending in the current tax year. A non-resident refers to a person who does not meet the test of residency above.

Salary includes salary, remunerations, indemnity, bonuses, overtime payments, compensations, and other payments in cash or in kind which are paid to the employee or paid for the direct or indirect benefit of the employee for employment services.

Resident taxpayers are subject to TOS at progressive rates from 0% to 20% while non-resident taxpayers are subject to a flat rate of 20%. Sub-Decree 09 provides the implementation of the new rate of the TOS as below. This implementation will take effect for salaries received from February 2020 onward:

The Monthly Salary Scale

Khmer Riel (KHR)	*USD*	*Tax Rate*
From KHR0–KHR1 300 000	0–325	0%
From KHR1 300 001–KHR2 000 000	325–500	5%
From KHR2 000 001–KHR8 500 000	500–2 125	10%
From KHR8 500 001–KHR12 500 000	2 125–3 125	15%
Over KHR12 500 000	Over 3 125	20%

In addition, a rebate of KHR150 000 is provided for every dependent child and spouse of the resident employee if:

(a) the dependent child is a minor, for which purpose the child must be 14 and under, or under 25 and a full-time student at an accredited institution.
(b) the only occupation of the employee's spouse is a homemaker (i.e., they do not work outside the home).

The employee must maintain the Family Book, Birth Certificate, Cambodian ID Card/Passport and Study Certificate of the dependent child for the tax officials to review during the tax audit session.

6. Tax on Fringe Benefits ("TOFB")

[306] Benefits in cash or kind provided to the employee are subject to the FBT at the flat rate of 20% of the market value of the benefit provided. Fringe benefits include:

(a) the use of motor vehicles;

(b) the provision of meals and accommodation support (including utilities and domestic helpers);
(c) low-interest loans and discounted sales;
(d) educational assistance (unless employment-related, for example, for training);
(e) educational assistance for the employee's children;
(f) certain insurance support where the same insurances are not available to every employee, irrespective of position;
(g) excessive unnecessary cash allowances, and social welfare in excess of the level provided in the law and pension contributions in excess of 10% of the employee's monthly salary exclusive of fringe benefits.
(h) payment for expenses for entertainment and leisure that are not directly related to employment; and
(i) provision of any shares or parts of a company's capital.

Fringe benefit is defined to include any goods, services, or other benefits in cash or in kind, provided directly or indirectly by an employer to a physical person for the purpose of employment activities. However, where any payment is made to an employee for business purposes the payment is not subject to the TOFB, subject to documentation requirements.

7. Public Lighting Tax (PLT)

[307] The PLT is an indirect tax imposed on the sale of alcohol and cigarettes, whether imported or domestically manufactured. The tax is at 3% of the taxable value (excluding VAT and PLT). The taxable value is usually the equivalent selling price (excluding VAT and PLT).

Please note that Prakas 976 which entered into force on October 9, 2017 brings a measure of downstream tax relief on secondary sales of Alcohol and Cigarettes. Prakas 976 reduced the tax base on the calculation of PLT to 20% of the selling price (excluding PLT and VAT) for secondary sales (excluding an importer or local producer).

If the LLC imports/sells alcoholic beverages and cigarettes, then the LLC must collect and pay the PLT to the GDT by the deadline.

8. Specific Tax on Certain Merchandise and Goods ("ST")

[308] The ST is imposed on a number of local and imported products and services. This tax applies to goods such as soft drinks, alcoholic beverages, cigarettes, and to certain services such as entertainment services, domestic and international air tickets, and telephone services. The rates range from 3% to 45%.

If the LLC imports the alcohol to Cambodia, the SP is payable at the time of importation with the General Department of Customs and Excise.

Other Taxes

9. Capital Gain Tax

[309] CGT was formally introduced in Cambodia under Prakas 346 on April 1, 2020. Under Prakas 346, both individual Cambodian resident taxpayers and individual/corporate Cambodian non-resident taxpayers are subject to CGT at the rate of 20% on gains made from the sale or transfer of capital. Cambodian corporate resident taxpayers are not subject to CGT under Prakas 346.

Prakas 346 defines the term "capital" which includes immovable property, finance leases, investment assets, goodwill, intellectual property, and foreign currency. The term "immovable property" refers to land, houses, or buildings and constructions erected on land as defined in the tax on Immovable Property regulations. Meanwhile, the term "Investment property" refers to stock, bonds, and securities issued by a private enterprise.

In addition, the term "capital gain" refers to taxable income resulting from the revenue received from the sale or transfer of capital less any allowable expenses. For the sale or transfer of capital other than immovable property, a taxpayer is required to use the actual expense method to calculate the capital gain.

Taxpayers are required to submit a prescribed tax return and pay capital gains to the GDT within three months after the capital gain has been triggered.

Please note that the implementation of Prakas 346 was initially set on July 1, 2020 but it was deferred to January 1, 2022 following the GDT Notification 24094 dated October 22, 2020. However, the GDT has recently issued Notification No. 4577 GDT dated March 9, 2022 which extends the implementation of Prakas 346 to January 1, 2024.

10. Immovable Property Tax

[310] Immovable Property tax of 0.1% per annum is levied on all immovable property with a value of more than KHR100 million (approximately USD25 000). Immovable property includes land, houses, buildings and other constructions built on land. The tax base is the market value determined by the Immovable Property Evaluation Commission less the threshold of USD25 000. The owner, possessor or beneficiary of the property is responsible for the payment of property tax to the GDT.

11. Unused Land Tax

[311] Unused land tax is imposed on a vacant block of land without any buildings or land on which there is only an abandoned building or buildings. In some cities or in some regions the tax is determined by the committee for evaluation of unused land. Please note that unused land tax must be paid by the owner on land that does not fall within the scope of Property Tax. This tax is imposed at a rate of 2% of the land's market value as determined every year by a committee for evaluation of unused land.

12. Patent Tax

[312] All business enterprises must register annually with the GDT and pay a standard "patent tax" or "business registration tax." This tax must be paid within fifteen working days from the company's registration and by March 31 of each financial year:

Self-Assessment Regime of Taxation	*Patent Tax Fee (in KHR)*	*Patent Tax Fee (in USD)*
Small Taxpayer	KHR400 000	USD100
Medium Taxpayer	KHR1 2 million	USD300
Large Taxpayer	KHR3 million or KHR5 million*	USD750 or USD1 250

Please note that if the annual turnover of a Large Taxpayer exceeds KHR10 billion (approximately USD2 5 million) then the patent tax payable will be USD1 250. Meanwhile, if the annual turnover of the Large Taxpayer is less than KHR10 billion (approximately USD2 5 million), the patent tax payable will be USD750.

A business enterprise that has many different business activities or locations must pay separate patent taxes corresponding to its various business activities and locations. If a taxpayer has a branch office, warehouse, factory or workshop with the same business objective but in a different location (i.e., a different city or province), the taxpayer is required to pay an additional patent tax fee of KHR3 million (USD750) to the tax authority where the branch office, warehouse, etc. is located.

13. Related Party Transactions

[313] Prakas 986 requires that Cambodian enterprises engaging in related party transactions must comply with the following requirements:

(a) an annual transfer pricing declaration, to be submitted together with the annual declaration on tax on income; and
(b) annual transfer pricing documentation, to be submitted upon request by the GDT.

The annual disclosure will be used by the tax authorities to identify taxpayers with significant related party transactions for review, auditing, and potential adjustments if transactions are found not to be at "arm's length." Put simply, the arm's length principle provides that the amount charged by one related party to another for a given product/service must be the same as if the parties were not related.

A related party is defined as one of the following:

(a) a member of the same immediate family;
(b) one enterprise is directly or indirectly entitled to 20% of the dividend in the direct capital of the other enterprise or equivalent voting rights in the taxpayer's Board of Directors; and
(c) a third-party enterprise or an individual possesses directly or indirectly at least 20% of the dividend in the direct capital of both enterprises or equivalent voting rights in the Board of Directors of both enterprises.

5.3 Tax Administration

[314] The following are the tax compliance requirements of a registered taxpayer:

Taxes	*Deadline*
Withholding Tax	20th day for manual filing or 25th for E-filing of the succeeding month
Tax on Salary and Fringe Benefit Tax	20th day for manual filing or 25th for E-filing day of the succeeding month
Prepayment Tax on Income	20th day for manual filing or 25th for E-filing of the succeeding month
Value-Added Tax	20th day for manual filing or 25th for E-filing of the succeeding month
Public Lighting Tax	20th day for manual filing or 25th for E-filing of the succeeding month
Annual Tax on Income/ Minimum Tax	Three months after year end
Patent Tax	March 31 of each year

Penalties

[315] Tax penalties are imposed for violations of the LOT and its regulations. The level of penalty is dependent upon the nature of the violation, and is determined as follows:

(a) where a taxpayer or withholding agent is considered negligent (where there is less than 10% underpayment of the taxes due) the amount of penalty will be 10% of the unpaid tax;
(b) where a taxpayer or withholding agent is considered seriously negligent (where the underpayment of the tax exceeds 10% or the taxpayer has failed to settle tax liabilities by the due date stated in the reminder letter issued by the GDT) the amount of penalty will be 25% of the unpaid tax; and
(c) where the taxpayer or withholding agent receives a unilateral tax assessment the amount of the penalty will be 40% of the unpaid tax.

Under Article 116 of the LOT, the GDT has the right to apply a unilateral tax assessment if the taxpayer:

(a) fails to submit a required return or declaration;

(b) fails to maintain proper records of account or any of the required documentation; and
(c) fails to provide information to the GDT when required to do so.

Penalties together with interest charged at 1.5% per month will apply for the late payment of taxes and late lodgement of returns.

5.4 Tax Considerations Arising on M&A Transactions

5.4.1 Share Acquisition

[316] From a Cambodian tax perspective, if the shares in the Cambodian entity are held by a non-resident or individual Cambodian tax resident shareholder, then any resulting capital gains are currently not taxed in Cambodia. Whilst the Cambodian tax regulations do contemplate the taxation of gains on a share transfer as falling under the TOI regime, there is currently no mechanism via which a non-resident shareholder is required to declare again unless they are required to be registered as a taxpayer in Cambodia. As noted above the tax authorities in Cambodia have recently tried to re-assess capital gains tax on historical share transfers by non-residents in Cambodian entities. The application of capital gains tax on share transfers is currently being discussed between the private sector and authorities.

[317] There is a stamp tax that applies to the transfer of shares in a Cambodian entity which is levied on the purchase of the shares at the rate of 0.1%. The stamp tax is levied on the "market value" of the shares that have been transferred which, in practice, is the higher of: (i) the actual consideration paid for the shares; (ii) the par value of the shares; or (iii) the net asset book value of the company from which the shares are transferred. The stamp tax is payable within ninety days after the share transfer has been executed.

[318] Given that the acquirer will be responsible for any historical undisclosed tax liabilities of the target, it is common for a purchaser of shares in a Cambodian entity to require the entity to undergo a comprehensive tax audit up to the date of share transfer so that the purchaser has a degree of comfort with respect to undisclosed tax liabilities. Practically speaking, the completion of a comprehensive tax audit can take some time, which means in some cases the use of an escrow account is required to defer partial payment of the share price until the tax clearance process has been completed.

[319] A change in shareholder continuity will not impact tax losses in a Cambodian entity.

[320] As noted above, Prakas 372 introduced in April 2019 may create a WHT implication on a deemed dividend distribution in the event that a non-resident shareholder transfers shares in a Cambodian entity that has retained earnings. In this scenario, the Cambodian entity whose shares are transferred will be required to withhold and pay WHT to the GDT by the 25th of the month following the MOC approval of the share transfer. In theory, the WHT imposition on the deemed dividend should be borne by the outgoing shareholder. However, for certainty, we suggest that the underlying share purchase agreement clearly outlines which party is to bear the cost of the WHT.

5.4.2 Business Transfer

[321] A business transfer or sale of a going concern involves the transfer of an existing business in Cambodia to another legal entity in Cambodia. Typically, a registered taxpayer in Cambodia would be required to charge 10% VAT on the transfer of any of its assets. Provided all the underlying criteria are met, a taxpayer transferring its business will not be required to charge 10% VAT.

[322] Article 82 of the LOT states:

> The transfer of a business from one person to another person, in accordance with the conditions to be provided by sub-decree, shall not be subject to the tax on value-added. The rule and procedures for the notification of transfer, the registration of the person acquiring the business, the responsibility of the person transferring the business, the responsibility of the person acquiring the business, and the preservation of records shall be determined by sub-decree.

[323] Further, the implementing sub-decree, namely Article 55 of the VAT Sub-Decree, states:

> The transfer of a business from one person to another person in accordance with the following conditions shall not be subject to value-added tax:
>
> (i) The business must be transferred from one person to another and continue trading in the new ownership.
> (ii) The taxable person transferring the business shall notify the Real Regime Tax Office of the transfer of the business within 10 days of the date of the transfer.
> (iii) The taxable person transferring the business shall seek cancellation of his registration, if appropriate, and shall comply with the provisions of Article 81 of the Law on Taxation and the relevant Articles of Chapter 5 of this Sub-Decree.
> (iv) The recipient of business shall be registered for VAT as a taxable person at the time the business is acquired and shall account for tax on the stock and assets acquired at the time of their supply.
> (v) The recipient of the business shall retain the tax records related to the business transferred for a period of 10 years, as stated in Article 98 of the Law on Taxation.

[324] Any gains made by the taxpayer on the transfer of business will be subject to the standard 20% TOI rate in Cambodia.

5.4.3 Merger

[325] There is very little guidance in the Cambodian tax regulations with respect to the tax implications of a merger. To date, there have been very few reported mergers in Cambodia. It is anticipated that the new Law on Taxation which is slated to come into effect in 2023 may contain some references to the tax implications of mergers in Cambodia.

www.ingramcontent.com/pod-product-compliance
Lightning Source LLC
Chambersburg PA
CBHW071357230926
51846CB00002B/579
9789403530178